Test-Driven JavaScript Development

Learn JavaScript test-driven development using popular frameworks and tools

Ravi Kumar Gupta

Hetal Prajapati

Harmeet Singh

PUBLISHING

BIRMINGHAM - MUMBAI

Test-Driven JavaScript Development

First published: December 2015

Production reference: 1141215

Published by Packt Publishing Ltd.
Livery Place
35 Livery Street
Birmingham B3 2PB, UK.

ISBN 978-1-78217-492-9

www.packtpub.com

Credits

Authors
Ravi Kumar Gupta

Hetal Prajapati

Harmeet Singh

Reviewers
Raiyan Kamal

Bohdan Liashenko

Hema Pandey

Commissioning Editor
Sarah Crofton

Acquisition Editor
Usha Iyer

Content Development Editor
Shali Deeraj

Technical Editor
Prajakta Mhatre

Copy Editor
Charlotte Carneiro

Project Coordinator
Sanchita Mandal

Proofreader
Safis Editing

Indexer
Tejal Daruwale Soni

Graphics
Kirk D'Penha

Jason Monteiro

Production Coordinator
Aparna Bhagat

Cover Work
Aparna Bhagat

About the Authors

Ravi Kumar Gupta is an open source software evangelist and Liferay expert. He pursued M.S. degree in software system from BITS Pilani and B.Tech from LNMIIT, Jaipur. His technological forte is portal management and development using Liferay along with popular JavaScript libraries.

He is currently working as a lead consultant with CIGNEX Datamatics. He was a core member of the open source group at TCS, where he started working on Liferay and other UI technologies. During his career, he has been involved in building enterprise solutions using latest technologies with rich user interfaces and open source tools.

He loves to spend time writing, learning, and discussing new technologies. He is an active member of the Liferay forum. He also writes technical articles for his blog at *TechD of Computer World* (`http://techdc.blogspot.in`). He has been a Liferay trainer at TCS and CIGNEX, where he has provided training on Liferay 5.x and 6.x versions. He was also a reviewer for the book *Learning Bootstrap* by Packt.

He can be reached on Skype at `kravigupta` and on Twitter at `@kravigupta`. Connect with him on LinkedIn at `http://in.linkedin.com/in/kravigupta`.

I would like to thank my lovely wife Kriti and my family for their tremendous support in tough times. All that I am is because of them. Their support has helped me through good and bad times.

Thank you so much my co-authors Hetal and Harmeet for excellent support, the Packt team for understanding and cooperation, and the reviewers and editorial team for providing the right feedback. I truly appreciate you guys.

Hetal Prajapati is a technical lead working with CIGNEX Datamatics. She is from Gandhinagar, the capital city of the vibrant state of Gujarat. She did her masters in IT from Dhirubhai Ambani Institute of Information and Communication Technology, Gandhinagar. Her expertise includes designing and developing solutions for Enterprise Content Management portals.

She has been involved in building enterprise solutions using Liferay and other open source technologies across different domains. She has been involved in imparting training for Liferay using Liferay 5.x and 6.x. Apart from Liferay, Hetal has also worked on many other technologies and frameworks, such as Java, MongoDB, Spring, Hibernate, jQuery, JavaScript, and AngularJS. She loves to listen to music and read books in her free time. She can be reached on Twitter at `@hetalp84`. You can also connect with her on LinkedIn at `http://in.linkedin.com/in/hetalprajapati`.

I would like to express gratitude for the support and help provided by the entire Packt Publishing team throughout this project.

I also like to thank my co-authors Ravi and Harmeet for their excellent support during the entire project. Finally, I wish to thank my parents, my husband Jayesh, and my son Prakhar for their support and encouragement throughout my project.

Harmeet Singh is a Sr. UI Developer working for Cignex Datamatics with varied experience in UI. He hails from the holy city of Amritsar, India. His expertise includes HTML5, JavaScript, jQuery, AngularJS, NodeJS, and more. His interests include music, sports, dancing, and adventures.

Harmeet has given various presentations and conducted workshops on UI development. On the academic front, Harmeet is a graduate in IT and a GNIIT diploma holder from NIIT specializing in software engineering. He can be reached on Skype at `harmeetsingh090`. You can also connect with him on LinkedIn at `https://in.linkedin.com/in/harmeetsingh090`.

I am really thankful to my colleagues Ravi, Hetal, and Nikhil whose support and encouragement led me to write this book and kept me motivated throughout the journey of completing this book. I am really thankful from the core of my heart to UI lead Mehul Bhatt and Vasim Khan for their immense contribution and guidelines.

About the Reviewers

Raiyan Kamal is a strong proponent of the open source movement and sporadically contributes to various open source projects. He holds a bachelor's degree in computer science from BUET, Dhaka, Bangladesh, and a master's degree from the UWindsor, Ontario, Canada. He has worked in the software industry for several years, developing software for mobile, web, and desktop platforms. He is currently working at IOU Concepts Inc., exploring different ways of saying "Thank you". When not doing stuffs on a computer, Raiyan plants trees and composts kitchen scraps.

Bohdan Liashenko has more than five years of experience in web development. He took part in the development of large projects for logistics, embedded solutions, and secure applications for enterprise. All of the projects he has been involved with were JavaScript-based. He has solid experience in design architecture and the development of complex HTML5 applications and practices high performance code optimization for JS and testing.

Currently he works as a technical lead at SoftServe Development Inc. Apart from this, he is the founder of the Imagine Dream Game studio and works on his own indie-game project.

Hema Pandey is a PMP-certified project manager with 8.5 years of total experience in the IT services and solutions industry in all phases of SDLC and project management. She completed her B.E. in computer science and engineering from Dehradun Institute of Technology and was placed in Tata Consultancy Services. She was associated with TCS for 7.5 years. Currently, she is working with Tavisca Solutions Pvt. Ltd since December 2014.

Her interests include wildlife photography, bird watching, mountaineering, and writing short stories and articles.

She can be reached on Skype at `pandeyhema399`. Connect with her on LinkedIn at `https://www.linkedin.com/in/hema-pandey-17b12216`.

www.PacktPub.com

Support files, eBooks, discount offers, and more

For support files and downloads related to your book, please visit www.PacktPub.com.

Did you know that Packt offers eBook versions of every book published, with PDF and ePub files available? You can upgrade to the eBook version at www.PacktPub. com and as a print book customer, you are entitled to a discount on the eBook copy. Get in touch with us at service@packtpub.com for more details.

At www.PacktPub.com, you can also read a collection of free technical articles, sign up for a range of free newsletters and receive exclusive discounts and offers on Packt books and eBooks.

https://www2.packtpub.com/books/subscription/packtlib

Do you need instant solutions to your IT questions? PacktLib is Packt's online digital book library. Here, you can search, access, and readPackt's entire library of books.

Why subscribe?

- Fully searchable across every book published by Packt
- Copy and paste, print, and bookmark content
- On demand and accessible via a web browser

Free access for Packt account holders

If you have an account with Packt atwww.PacktPub.com, you can use this to access PacktLib today and view 9 entirely free books. Simply use your login credentials for immediate access.

Table of Contents

Preface

Initially, all processing used to happen on the server's side and simple output was the response to web browsers. Nowadays, there are so many JavaScript frameworks and libraries that help readers to create charts, animations, simulations, and so on. By the time a project finishes or reaches a stable state, so much JavaScript code has already been written that changing and maintaining it further is tedious. At this point comes the importance of automated testing, and more specifically, developing all that code in a test-driven environment. Test-driven development is a methodology that makes testing the central part of the design process—before writing code, developers decide upon the conditions that code must meet to pass a test. The end goal is to help the readers understand the importance and process of using TDD as a part of the development.

This book starts with the details of test-driven development, its importance, need, and benefits. Later, the book introduces popular tools and frameworks, such as YUI, Karma, QUnit, DalekJS, JsUnit, and so on, to utilize Jasmine, Mocha, and Karma for advanced concepts such as feature detection, server-side testing, and patterns. We are going to understand, write, run tests, and further debug our programs. The book concludes with best practices in JavaScript testing. By the end of the book, the readers will know why they should test, how to do it most efficiently, and will have a number of versatile tests (and methods to devise new tests) so they can get to work immediately.

What this book covers

Chapter 1, *Overview of TDD*, introduces the test-driven development, its life cycle, benefits, and myths.

Chapter 2, *Testing Concepts*, brings the TDD life cycle into action using Yahoo User Interface (YUI) Tests, and explains how unit testing can be done for JavaScript.

Chapter 3, Testing Tools, introduces JsUnit, QUnit, Karma, and DalekJS, which are some of the popular unit testing frameworks for JavaScript.

Chapter 4, Jasmine, introduces behavior-driven development and the Jasmine framework, its setup, usage, and customization, along with several features that a good unit testing framework should cover.

Chapter 5, JsTestDriver, showcases the JsTestDriver unit testing tool and its integration with IDE.

Chapter 6, Feature Detection, explores has.js and Modernizr JavaScript libraries for feature detection and explains why feature detection should have preference over browser detection.

Chapter 7, Observer Design Pattern, explains the observer pattern for JavaScript and its role in the test-driven development.

Chapter 8, Testing with Server-Side JS, covers server-side JavaScript unit testing using Node.js, Mocha, and Chai while using MongoDB as a database.

Chapter 9, Best Practices, lists best practices used to unit test JavaScript and also helps to make a good choice among popular unit testing frameworks and tools by explaining the features.

What you need for this book

To run the examples included in this book, the following tools will be required:

YUI Test	3.18.1	http://yuilibrary.com/yui/docs/test/
JsUnit	2.2	http://sourceforge.net/projects/jsunit/files/
		https://github.com/pivotal/jsunit
QUnit	1.18.0	http://code.jquery.com/qunit/
Node.js	0.10.29	http://blog.nodejs.org/2014/06/16/node-v0-10-29-stable/
		http://nodejs.org
Karma	0.12.32	Node package
Dalek	0.0.5	Node package
DalekJS	0.0.9	http://dalekjs.com/
Jasmine	2.3.0, 1.1.0	https://github.com/jasmine/jasmine/releases

JsTestDriver	1.3.5	`https://code.google.com/p/js-test-driver/` `downloads/detail?name=JsTestDriver-1.3.5.jar` `http://js-test-driver.googlecode.com/svn/` `update`
Eclipse	Indigo	`http://www.eclipse.org/downloads/download.` `php?file=/technology/epp/downloads/` `release/indigo/SR2/eclipse-jee-indigo-SR2-` `win32-x86_64.zip`
Jasmine-jstd-adapter		`https://github.com/ibolmo/jasmine-jstd-adapter`
lcov		`https://github.com/linux-test-project/lcov`
Cygwin		`https://cygwin.com/install.html`
has.js		`https://github.com/phiggins42/has.js`
Modernizr	3	`https://github.com/Modernizr/Modernizr` `http://modernizr.com/download/`
Mocha	2.3.3	`Installed as node package`
MongoDB	3.0.6	`https://www.mongodb.org/downloads#production`
Chai	3.3.0	`Installed as node package`

Who this book is for

If you have an intermediate knowledge of HTML, CSS, and JavaScript and want to learn how and why the test-driven development approach is better for your assignments, then this book is for you.

Conventions

In this book, you will find a number of text styles that distinguish between different kinds of information. Here are some examples of these styles and an explanation of their meaning.

Code words in text, database table names, folder names, filenames, file extensions, pathnames, dummy URLs, user input, and Twitter handles are shown as follows: "This will start a server on port 9880 keeping runner mode QUIET as you can see in the command prompt after running the command."

A block of code is set as follows:

```
<script>
YUI().use('test-console','test', function (Y) {
    var testCase = new Y.Test.Case({
      /*
      * Sets up data needed by each test.
```

When we wish to draw your attention to a particular part of a code block, the relevant lines or items are set in bold:

```
toCurrencyAmount = rateOfConversion* amount;

// rounding off
toCurrencyAmount = Number.parseFloat(toCurrencyAmount).toFixed(2);
```

Any command-line input or output is written as follows:

```
npm install karma -save-dev
```

New terms and **important words** are shown in bold. Words that you see on the screen, for example, in menus or dialog boxes, appear in the text like this: "Click on the first link **Capture This Browser**, which will allow JsTestDriver to capture this browser."

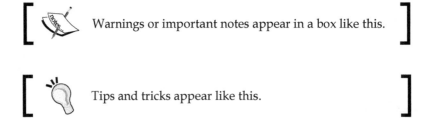

Warnings or important notes appear in a box like this.

Tips and tricks appear like this.

Reader feedback

Feedback from our readers is always welcome. Let us know what you think about this book—what you liked or disliked. Reader feedback is important for us as it helps us develop titles that you will really get the most out of.

To send us general feedback, simply e-mail feedback@packtpub.com, and mention the book's title in the subject of your message.

If there is a topic that you have expertise in and you are interested in either writing or contributing to a book, see our author guide at www.packtpub.com/authors.

Customer support

Now that you are the proud owner of a Packt book, we have a number of things to help you to get the most from your purchase.

Downloading the example code

You can download the example code files from your account at http://www.packtpub.com for all the Packt Publishing books you have purchased. If you purchased this book elsewhere, you can visit http://www.packtpub.com/support and register to have the files e-mailed directly to you.

Errata

Although we have taken every care to ensure the accuracy of our content, mistakes do happen. If you find a mistake in one of our books—maybe a mistake in the text or the code—we would be grateful if you could report this to us. By doing so, you can save other readers from frustration and help us improve subsequent versions of this book. If you find any errata, please report them by visiting http://www.packtpub.com/submit-errata, selecting your book, clicking on the **Errata Submission Form** link, and entering the details of your errata. Once your errata are verified, your submission will be accepted and the errata will be uploaded to our website or added to any list of existing errata under the Errata section of that title.

To view the previously submitted errata, go to https://www.packtpub.com/books/content/support and enter the name of the book in the search field. The required information will appear under the **Errata** section.

Piracy

Piracy of copyrighted material on the Internet is an ongoing problem across all media. At Packt, we take the protection of our copyright and licenses very seriously. If you come across any illegal copies of our works in any form on the Internet, please provide us with the location address or website name immediately so that we can pursue a remedy.

Please contact us at copyright@packtpub.com with a link to the suspected pirated material.

We appreciate your help in protecting our authors and our ability to bring you valuable content.

Questions

If you have a problem with any aspect of this book, you can contact us at questions@packtpub.com, and we will do our best to address the problem.

Overview of TDD 1

There are several ways to develop a project. Testing is one of the most important phases in the development of any project, and in the traditional software development model, it is usually executed after the code for functionality is written. **Test-driven development** (**TDD**) makes a big difference by writing tests before the actual code.

You are going to learn TDD for JavaScript and see how this approach can be utilized in projects. In this chapter, you are going to learn the following:

- The complexity of web pages
- Understanding TDD
- Agile and TDD
- Benefits of TDD and common myths

Complexity of web pages

When Tim Berners-Lee wrote the first ever web browser around 1990, it was supposed to run HTML, neither CSS nor JavaScript. Who knew that WWW will be the most powerful communication medium? Since then, there are now a number of technologies and tools that help us write the code and run it for our needs. We do a lot these days with the help of the Internet. We shop, read, learn, share, and collaborate... well, a few words are not going to suffice to explain what we do on the Internet, are they? Over the period of time, our needs have grown to a very complex level, so is the complexity of code written for websites. It's not plain HTML anymore, not some CSS style, not some basic JavaScript tweaks. That time has passed. Pick any site you visit daily, view source by opening developer tools of the browser, and look at the source code of the site. What do you see? Too much code? Too many styles? Too many scripts? The JavaScript code and CSS code is so huge to keep it as inline, and we need to keep them in different files, sometimes even different folders to keep them organized.

Now, what happens before you publish all the code live? You test it. You test each line and see if that works fine. Well, that's a programmer's job. Zero defect, that's what every organization tries to achieve. When that is in focus, testing comes into the picture, more importantly a development style that is essentially test driven. As the title for this book says, we're going to keep our focus on test-driven JavaScript development.

Understanding test-driven development

TDD, short for test-driven development, is a process for software development. Kent Beck, who is known for development of TDD, refers to this as "rediscovery." Someone asked a question (Why does Kent Beck refer to the "rediscovery" of test-driven development?) about this. Kent's answer to this question on Quora can be found at `https://www.quora.com/Why-does-Kent-Beck-refer-to-the-rediscovery-of-test-driven-development`.

> *"The original description of TDD was in an ancient book about programming. It said you take the input tape, manually type in the output tape you expect, then program until the actual output tape matches the expected output. After I'd written the first xUnit framework in Smalltalk I remembered reading this and tried it out. That was the origin of TDD for me. When describing TDD to older programmers, I often hear, "Of course. How else could you program?" Therefore I refer to my role as "rediscovering" TDD."*

If you go and try to find references to TDD, you would even get few references from 1968. However It's not a new technique, though it did not get so much attention at that time. Recently, an interest in TDD has been growing, and as a result there are a number of tools on the Web. For example, Jasmine, Mocha, DalekJS, JsUnit, QUnit, and Karma are among these popular tools and frameworks. More specifically, test-driven JavaScript development is becoming popular these days.

Test-driven development is a software development process, which enforces a developer to write a test before production code. A developer writes a test, expects a behavior, and writes code to make the test pass. It is needless to mention that the test will always fail at the start. You will learn more about the life cycle later in this chapter.

The need for testing

To err is human. As a developer, it's not easy to find defects in our own code, and often we think that our code is perfect. But there is always a chance that a defect is present in the code. Every organization or individual wants to deliver the best software they can. This is one major reason that every software, every piece of code is well tested before its release. Testing helps to detect and correct defects.

There are a number of reasons why testing is needed. They are as follows:

- To check if the software is functioning as per the requirements
- There will not be just one device or one platform to run your software
- The end users sometimes perform an action as a programmer that you never expected, and these actions might result in defects. To catch these defects, we need testing

There was a study conducted by the **National Institute of Standards and Technology (NIST)** in 2002, which reported that software bugs cost the U.S. economy around $60 billion annually. With better testing, more than one-third of the cost could be avoided. The earlier the defect is found, the cheaper it is to fix it. A defect found post release would cost 10-100 times more to fix than if it had already been detected and fixed pre-release.

The report on the study performed by NIST can be found at `http://www.nist.gov/director/planning/upload/report02-3.pdf`.

If we draw a curve for the cost, it comes as an exponential. The following figure clearly shows that the cost increases as the project matures with time. Sometimes, it's not possible to fix a defect without making changes in the architecture. In those cases, the cost is sometimes so great that developing the software from scratch seems like a better option.

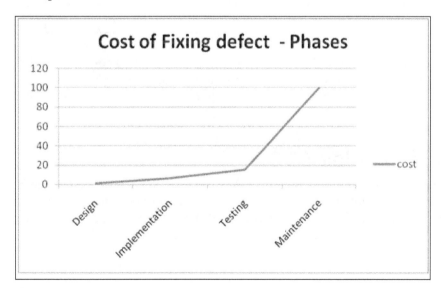

Types of testing

Any product, website, or utility, should be very well tested before it is launched. There are a number of testing techniques used to test software. From a block of code to system integration testing, every kind of testing is performed for a zero-defect system. Test-driven development is more about unit testing. It helps to learn about defects in a system at a very early stage. You will learn more about unit tests and testing concepts in the next chapter.

The following figure shows the cost of detecting and fixing defects in different testing types:

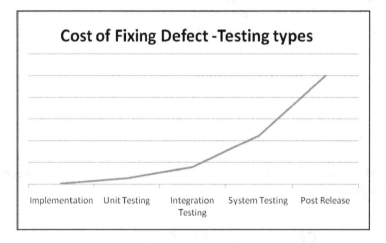

As we can clearly see, if unit testing is performed, the cost of correcting a defect is close to correcting defects at the time of implementation. Since TDD enforces writing unit tests, the cost of the overall project is reduced significantly by reducing the number of defects after release.

The life cycle of TDD

The life cycle of TDD can be divided into several steps. Each time a change is to be made into the system, tests cases are written first and then some code to make the tests pass, and so on. Let's get a closer look at the life cycle. See the following figure:

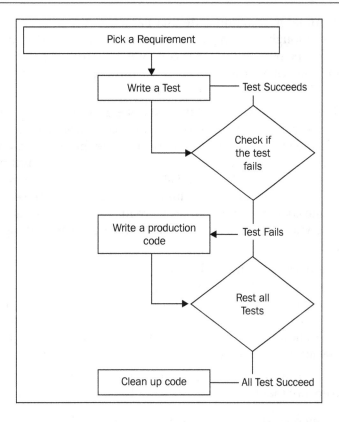

The different phases of the life cycle of TDD can be explained as follows:

- **Write a test**: After a set of requirements is captured, one requirement is picked and tests are written for that. Implementation of every new feature or every change begins with writing tests for it. The test can also be a modified version of an existing one.

  This is a major difference between TDD versus other techniques, where unit tests are written after the code is written. This makes the developer focus on the requirements before writing the code. This also makes it a test-first development approach.

- **Run the test and see if the test fails**: A new test should always require some code to be written to make it pass. This step validates that the new test should not pass without requiring new code. This also verifies whether the required feature already exists or not. This step helps the developer increase confidence that the unit test is testing the correct constraint, and passes only in the intended cases.

- **Write minimal production code that passes**: In this step, the developer writes just enough code to pass the test. The code written in this stage is not supposed to be perfect. Since the code will be improved and cleaned at a later stage, the code as of now is acceptable. At this point, the only purpose of the written code is to pass the test.

- **Run all tests**: Now, we run all the test cases at once. If every test passes, the programmer can be confident that the new code works as required and does not break any existing functionality or degrade the system anyhow. If any of the tests fail, the new code must be corrected to make the test pass. Usually, all our tests should be atomic and should not fail even if a new code is added, but that's not always the case. It may happen that someone else in the team added some code or some changes were made to the existing code. So, it's always a good practice to run all tests to make sure everything works fine as it should have.

- **The cleanup code**: At the end of development, there would be thousands of such test cases and code base that grows and can become complex if it is not cleaned up regularly. Refactoring is much needed. Duplicate code must be removed. Variables, functions, and so on should follow standards, and names should clearly represent their purpose and use. Code comments should be added for readability and documentation purpose.

  Removal of duplicate code applies to both production and test code. It is a must to ensure that refactoring does not break any existing features.

- **Repeat**: The preceding steps give a somewhat stable code in just one iteration, which works for some defined functionalities. The whole process is now repeated for another requirement. In case new tests fail, the developer can revert the changes or undo the operation performed. This gives a rapid feedback to the developer about the progress and problems in the system.

TDD microcycle

The TDD life cycle is also defined as **Red-Green-Refactor**, which is also called as the microcycle.

This process can be illustrated as shown in the following figure:

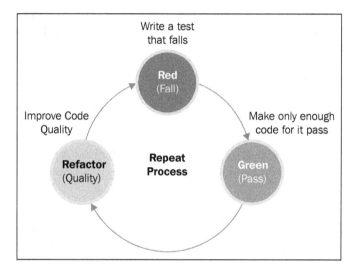

There are only three steps in this microcycle:

- **Write a test that fails at the start (Red)**: First of all, simple test cases are written, which test the code yet to be implemented. At this step, the test will always fail (In the figure, it has been colored red).

- **Write just enough code to pass the test (Green)**: The developer then writes the code to pass the test. The code is written in the simplest manner and is just sufficient to pass the test.

- **Refactor the code (Refactor)**: Before implementing a new feature, developers refactor the old code, which just passed, for clarity and simplicity. This step improves the code quality.

This microcycle provides rapid feedback to the developer. As soon as a change is made to the system, it is tested. If there is any error, it's detected as soon as possible and fixed.

Agile and TDD

When we talk about TDD, Agile is most often discussed. Sometimes, people have doubts about whether Agile can exist without TDD or not. Well, of course it can, though. Agile and some people would say that TDD is Agile at a bigger scale. Through TDD, both show similar characteristics, but they are different. Agile is a process where testing is done as soon as a component is developed. It's not necessary in Agile to write test cases first and then perform development. But in the case of TDD, a test is always written first, and then its corresponding minimal production code.

TDD is about how code should be written while Agile is about the whole development process, not just code and its testing. Agile does not tell you how to build the system. Agile methodology is a management process, which can use TDD as an integral part.

Agile, when combined in practice with TDD, brings the best results. This combination minimizes risks, defects, cost, and results in a nearly zero-defect system.

Benefits of TDD and common myths

Every methodology has its own benefits and myths. The following sections will analyze the key benefits and most common myths of TDD.

Benefits

TDD has its own advantages over regular development approaches. There are a number of benefits, which help in making a decision of using TDD over the traditional approach.

- **Automated testing**: If you have seen a website code, you know that it's not easy to maintain and test all the scripts manually and keep them working. A tester may leave a few checks, but automated tests won't. Manual testing is error-prone and slow.

- **Lower cost of overall development**: With TDD, the number of debugs is significantly decreased. You develop some code, run tests; if you fail, re-doing the development is significantly faster than debugging and fixing it. TDD aims at detecting defect and correcting them at an early stage, which costs much less than detecting and correcting at a later stage or post release.

  Also, now debugging is much less frequent and a significant amount of time is saved. With the help of tools/test runners like Karma, JSTestDriver, and so on, running every JavaScript tests on browser is not needed, which saves significant time in validation and verification while the development goes on.

- **Increased productivity**: Apart from time and financial benefits, TDD helps to increase productivity since the developer becomes more focused and tends to write quality code that passes and fulfills the requirement.

- **Clean, maintainable, and flexible code**: Since tests are written first, production code is often very neat and simple. When a new piece of code is added, all the tests can be run at once to see if anything failed with the change.

  Since we try to keep our tests atomic, and our methods also address a single goal, the code automatically becomes clean.

  At the end of the application development, there will be thousands of test cases, which will guarantee that every piece of logic can be tested.

> The same test cases also act as documentation for users who are new to the development of the system, since these tests act as an example of how the code works.

- **Improved quality and reduced bugs**: Complex codes invite bugs. when developers change anything in neat and simple code, they tend to leave fewer or no bugs at all. They tend to focus on the purpose and write code to fulfill the requirement.

- **Keeps technical debt to minimum**: This is one of the major benefits of TDD. Not writing unit tests and documentation is a big part, as this increases the technical debt for a software/project. Since TDD encourages you to write tests first, and if they are well written they act as documentation, you keep the technical debt for these to a minimum.

  As Wikipedia says, "A technical debt can be defined as tasks to be performed before a unit can be called complete. If the debt is not repaid, interest also adds up and makes it harder to make changes at a later stage". More about technical debt can be found at `https://en.wikipedia.org/wiki/Technical_debt`.

Myths

Along with the benefits, TDD has some myths as well. Let's check few of them:

- **Complete code coverage**: TDD forces the writing of tests first, developers write the minimum amount of code to pass the test, and almost 100% code coverage is achieved. But that does not guarantee that nothing has been missed and the code is bug free. Code coverage tools do not cover all the paths. There can be infinite possibilities in loops. Of course it's not possible and feasible to check all the paths, but a developer is supposed to take care of major and critical paths.

  A developer is supposed to take care of business logic, flow, and process code most of the time. There is no need to test integration parts, setter-getter methods for properties, configurations, UI, and so on. Mocking and stubbing is to be used for integrations.

- **No need of debugging the code**: Though test-first development makes one think that debugging is not needed, but it's not always true. You need to know the state of the system when a test failed. That will help you to correct and further develop the code.

- **No need for QA**: TDD cannot always cover everything. QA plays a very important role in testing. UI defects, integration defects, are more likely to be caught by a QA. Even though developers are excellent, there are chances for errors. QA will try every kind of input and unexpected behavior that even a programmer would not cover with test cases. They will always try to crash the system with random inputs, and discover defects.

- **I can code faster without tests and can also validate for zero defect**: While this may stand true for very small software and websites where the code is small and writing test cases may increase the overall time of development and delivery of the product. But for bigger products, it helps a lot to identify defects at a very early stage and provides a chance to correct them at a very low cost. As seen in the previous screenshots of the cost of fixing defects for phases and testing types, the cost of correcting a defect increases with time. Truly, whether TDD is required for a project or not depends on context.

- **TDD ensures good design and architecture**: TDD encourages developers to write quality code, but it is not a replacement for good design practice and quality code. Will a team of developers be enough to ensure a stable and scalable architecture? Design should still be done by following the standard practices.

- **You need to write all tests first**: Another myth says that you need to write all of the tests first and then the actual production code. Actually, generally an iterative approach is used. Write some tests first, then some code, run the tests, fix the code, run the tests, write more tests, and so on. With TDD, you always test parts of software and keep developing.

There are many myths, and covering all of them is not possible. The point is, TDD offers developers a better opportunity to deliver quality code. TDD helps organizations by delivering close to zero-defect products.

Summary

In this chapter, you learned about what TDD is. You got to know about the life cycle of TDD and how it is called test-first development. Later on, you learned about the benefits and myths of TDD.

In the next chapter, you will learn the concepts of unit testing, and how to write unit tests and run them.

2

Testing Concepts

There are a number of ways and methods to test software quality. TDD is focused on testing the small pieces of code using unit tests. Unit tests play a big and important role in TDD irrespective of the programming language. While learning TDD, it is essential to understand unit testing and testing frameworks. In the previous chapter, you learned about the life cycle of TDD. Now with examples, we will see how each step of the life cycle is executed. For this chapter, we will try to showcase examples using **YUI** (short for **Yahoo User Interface**) because of its simplicity and easy-to-understand functions.

In this chapter, you will learn about unit testing, a little about frameworks, how a test is written, actions, and assertions in unit tests. In this chapter, you will learn the following:

- Unit testing
- Following the process
- Benefits and pitfalls

Unit testing

Unit test is a function or method, which invokes a unit of module in software and checks assumptions about the system that the developer has in mind. Unit test helps the developer test the logical functionality of any module.

In other words, a unit is the testable piece of software. It can have more than one input and normally a single output. Sometimes, we treat a module of a system as a unit.

Unit test is only relevant to developers who are closely working with the code. A unit test is only applicable to test a logical piece of a code. Illogical code would not be tested with the use of unit testing. For example, getting and setting values in text field will not be considered in logical code.

Usually, the first unit test is harder to write for any developer. The first test requires more time for any developer. We should follow a practice of asking questions before writing the initial unit test. For example, should you use an already available unit test framework or write you own custom code? What about an automated build process? How about collecting, displaying, and tracking unit test code coverage? Developers are already less motivated to write any unit tests, and having to deal with these questions only makes the process more painful. However, the good thing is that once you're familiar with unit testing and you are comfortable with TDD, it makes life so much easier than before.

Unit testing frameworks

Unit testing frameworks help developers write, run, and review unit tests. These frameworks are commonly named as xUnit frameworks and share a set of features across implementations. Many times it happens that the developer has unknowingly written few unit tests, but those are not in structured unit testing. Whenever we open developer/development tools in a browser (for example, firebug in Firefox, Safari's Inspector, or others) and open console to debug your code, you probably write few statements and inspect the results printed in the console. In many cases, this is a form of unit testing, but these are not automated tests and the developer will not be able to use them again and again.

Usually, every developer has a practice to use some or the other framework when they use JavaScript in their system, likewise to write a unit test, we can use testing frameworks available in market. Testing frameworks provide a lot of the ready-made piece of code, that the developer does not need to recreate: test suite/case aggregation, assertions, mock/stub helpers, asynchronous testing implementation, and more. Plenty of good open source testing frameworks are available. We will use the YUI Test in this chapter, but of course all good practices are applicable across all frameworks—only the syntax (and maybe some semantics) differs.

The most important step for any testing framework is collecting all the tests into suites and test cases. Test suites and test cases are part of many files; each test file typically contains tests for a single module. Normally, grouping all tests for a module in one test suite is considered as the best practice. The suite can contain many test cases; each test case includes testing of small aspects of any module. Using setUp and tearDown functions provided at the suite and test-case levels, you can easily handle any pretest setup and post-test teardown, such as resetting the state of a database. Sometimes, setUp and tearDown functions are referred to as follows:

- beforeEach(): This function runs before each test.
- afterEach(): This function runs after each test.
- before(): This function runs before all tests. Executes only once.
- after(): This function runs after all tests. Executes only once.

setUp is usually called before running any test. When we want to run few statements before running test, we need to specify that in the setUp() method. For example, if we want to set some global variables, which is needed by test, then we can initialize those in the setUp() method. On the other hand, tearDown can be useful to clean up things after finishing your test, for example, if you want to reset a variable to some default value after test run is complete. We will understand this in more detail later on in this chapter.

YUI Tests

YUI stands for Yahoo! User Interface, which has a component YUI Test. It is a testing framework to unit test your JavaScript code. You will be learning more about how to use this library while practicing TDD life cycle in this chapter.

This library is available at http://yuilibrary.com/yui/docs/test/. You can use YUI Test library using http://yui.yahooapis.com/3.18.1/build/yui/yui-min.js, which is a minified version of this library.

Following the process

We have been talking about TDD and its life cycle in the last chapter. It's time to see it in action. In this section, we'll take a simple requirement and work on it to understand the life cycle. We will run the test in browser, see, and analyze the report.

Let's take an example of a currency converter. This is a very simple business requirement where the converter will take a conversion rate and amount as input and return the converted amount. We will build this requirement step by step. Recalling the screenshot in *Chapter 1, Overview of TDD*, for TDD life cycle, is as follows:

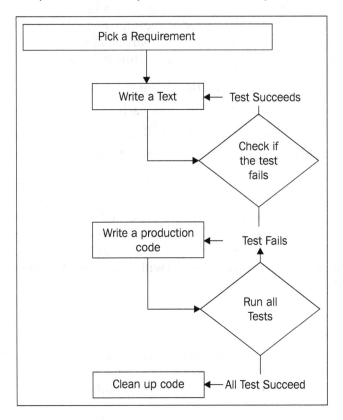

We will follow each life cycle step with an example to understand how tests are written and executed.

Preparing the environment

There are a number of frameworks and tools that we can use to write a unit test. For now, we are using YUI as mentioned before. We will write a simple HTML file, which includes JavaScript from YUI. We are going to use CSS for our test runner using the style located at `http://yui.yahooapis.com/2.9.0/build/logger/assets/skins/sam/logger.css` and YUI Test library from `http://yui.yahooapis.com/3.18.1/build/yui/yui-min.js`.

In general, you should always keep your business logic and tests in different files. For the sake of simplicity, we are keeping all code in one file for now. Let's take a very simple example of currency conversion. We will create a function which converts a given currency to another.

A simple file with no tests in it will be as follows:

```html
<!DOCTYPE html>
<html>
<head>
  <meta charset="UTF-8">
  <title>Chapter - 1</title>

  <link rel="stylesheet" type="text/css"
   href="http://yui.yahooapis.com/2.9.0/build/logger
   /assets/skins/sam/logger.css">

  <script src="http://yui.yahooapis.com/3.18.1/build/yui/yui-
    min.js"></script>
  <script>

    function convertCurrency(amount, rateOfConversion){
      // Business logic to convert currency
    }

    YUI().use('test-console', function (Y) {
      // ... all the tests go here ...

      // This will render a test console in the browser
      // in the container(div here) with id testLogs.
      new Y.Test.Console().render('#testLogs');

      // run the tests
      Y.Test.Runner.run();
    });
  </script>
</head>

<body class="yui3-skin-sam">
  <div id="testLogs">

  </div>
</body>
</html>
```

Let's see what the code is doing. We used the `YUI().use()` function in which we are utilizing the `test-console` module of YUI. We used the `new` keyword to create a new console on `div` with ID `testLog` using `new Y.Test.Console().render('#testLogs')`.

After rendering the test console, we try to run the tests using `Y.Test.Runner.run()`.

Let's run this code using test runner on the browser. We used Firefox for running the HTML file:

The test console is now blank since there is no test written and run yet. The included JavaScript file will load the YUI library, which will enable us to write the test cases and run them. This library will help us to print the test results into the console. This log can be printed to the console of the browser or to the test console provided by YUI. The CSS file is for styling the test console, which we will see very soon after creating a test and running it.

We have multiple options to display logs within the test console. We can opt to display different types of messages by selecting checkboxes. The types are info, pass, fail, and status.

Following the life cycle

We have already picked our requirement that we are going to write a piece of code for currency conversion. Let's follow the life cycle by writing a test.

Writing a test

We will name our function `convertCurrency()`. As of now, our function will not have an implementation. But our test will be present at this moment. Let's take an example of conversion. We will try to convert INR100 to USD. We are given that 1 USD = 63 INR. The result of conversion comes to 1.587. If we round it off to 2 decimal points, it's 1.59. Now we have all required input and desired output for a test. Let's write the test then.

After writing a test, our `<script>` tag will be as follows:

```
<script>
    // All our functions and tests go here.
    function convertCurrency(amount, rateOfConversion){
      var toCurrencyAmount = 0;
      return toCurrencyAmount;
    }

    YUI().use('test-console', function (Y) {
      var testCase = new Y.Test.Case({
        testCurrencyConversion: function () {
      var expectedResult = 1.59;
      var actualResult = convertCurrency(100, 1/63);

          Y.Assert.areEqual(expectedResult, actualResult,
          "100 INR should be equal to $ 1.59");
      }
    });

      //   Using YUI Test console.
      new Y.Test.Console({
        newestOnTop: false,
        width:"400px",
        height:"300px"
      }).render('# testLogs');

      Y.Test.Runner.add(testCase);
      //run all tests
      Y.Test.Runner.run();
    });
</script>
```

As of now, we have a dummy implementation of the `convertCurrency()` function with two parameters, one is the amount to be converted and the other is the rate of conversion. We added a test using new `Y.Test.Case()`. We created a function named `testCurrencyConversion` and added a line with an assertion call to `Y.Assert.areEqual()`. This method takes an expected value, actual value, or expression that will evaluate the actual value and an optional message, which can be printed when this test fails. Assertions are used as a checkpoint in our code to verify the trueness of our code. Here, we are checking if the value returned by the `convertCurrency()` function is correct or not by matching the output to the given value. You will learn more about assertions later in this chapter.

Running the test and seeing if test fails

Running this code will run our test and all messages will be put into the test console. If you note the preceding code, we used few properties while creating a test using new `Y.Test.Console()`. We used these to set the height and width of the test console. Let's run the file now:

You can see from the result that the test failed. It shows the message we added. It also shows the expected value and actual value and their types. TestRunner created a number of messages, but for now, we see only info and fail messages. Let's select **pass** and **status** checkboxes as well and take a look at all the other messages:

If you note the messages in the last run, you will see that TestRunner created a test suite for us and runs the test suite. Test suite is a collection of tests, which will run one by one when the test suite runs. You will learn more about test suites later in this chapter.

Writing a production code

Now when we already have the test, we know what is required to pass the test—a logic to calculate the converted currency amount. Let's take a look at the following code:

```
<script>
  // All our functions and tests go here.
  function convertCurrency(amount, rateOfConversion){
    var toCurrencyAmount = 0;
```

```
    // conversion
    toCurrencyAmount = rateOfConversion* amount;

    // rounding off
    toCurrencyAmount = Number.parseFloat(toCurrencyAmount).toFixed(2);

    return toCurrencyAmount;
}

YUI().use('test-console', function (Y) {
  var testCase = new Y.Test.Case({
    testCurrencyConversion: function () {
        var expectedResult = 1.59;
        var actualResult = convertCurrency(100, 1/63);

        Y.Assert.areEqual(expectedResult, actualResult, "100 INR
        should be equal to $ 1.59");
    }
  });

  //   Using YUI Test console.
  new Y.Test.Console({
    filters: {
      fail : true,
      pass : true
    },
    newestOnTop: false,
    width:"400px",
    height:"300px"
  }).render('# testLogs');

  Y.Test.Runner.add(testCase);
  //run all tests
  Y.Test.Runner.run();
});
</script>
```

We provided a simple implementation for our requirement—our production code. If we run this code using TestRunner on Firefox or Chrome, the test will pass. But IE does not support `Number.parseFloat()` and will fail the test:

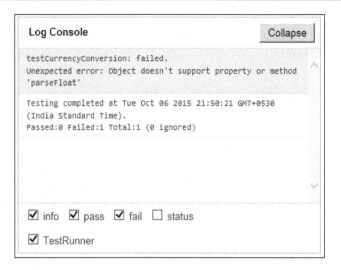

We need to check what should be the correct code for Internet Explorer. Let's correct the code to use global `parseFloat()` instead of `Number.parseFloat()`.

```
toCurrencyAmount = parseFloat(toCurrencyAmount).toFixed(2);
```

Please note that we added filters for **pass, fail** as true for console. Now the console will show fail and pass messages by default, and we don't need to check fail and pass in the UI.

Running all tests

Now that the implementation is done, let's run the tests again and look at what happens. Look at the following screenshot after running the tests:

Our test is passed. At this point, we have only one test to run, but that is not the case while developing a project. There may be a good amount of tests already prepared. Our new implementation may cause failure of tests, which already passed. In this case, you will need to recheck your code and fix the implementation until all tests pass. This will ensure that our new implementation never breaks any code that is previously written and all tests passed for.

Cleaning up the code

If all tests are passed in the previous step, we must clean and refactor the code. This is a very necessary step since there would be thousands of tests, if we don't clean up, we may end up with duplicate code, unnecessary variables, unnecessary statements, and code will never be optimized. Code comments or logs must be added for readability purpose. Believe it or not, code comments help a lot in understanding the code when you revisit the code after months.

Repeat

After cleaning up the code, we pick a requirement again and repeat the whole process and keep going. All this ensures that whatever you developed so far, works as expected.

Using the browser console

So far, you should have an understanding of how you can write a basic test and run it in the browser to see the logs in test console or browser's log console. There will be times when you won't be using test console to show your tests reports and you need to rely on browsers logs. In this case, simply remove the test console from the code and re-run the tests. Take a look at the following screenshot:

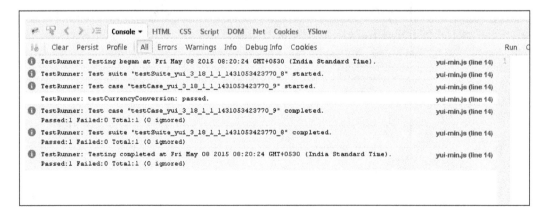

This is a console of Firebug plugin of the Firefox web browser. You would find similar logs in console of the Google Chrome web browser. To open the console in Chrome, press *Ctrl* + *Shift* + *I* in Microsoft Windows or *command* + *option* + *I* in Mac and look for the **Console** tab.

setUp() and tearDown()

When you need to set up some data before a test runs, you use the `setUp()` function. Likewise, to clear, delete, and terminate connections, which should happen at the end of the test, you use the `tearDown()` function. These functions may have different names in other testing frameworks/tools. Both of these methods are optional, and they will be used only when they are defined.

An example may be to set some initial data and use the data in the test. Let's check out the following code, which showcases a very simple implementation of the `setUp()` and `tearDown()` functions:

```
<script>
YUI().use('test-console','test', function (Y) {
    var testCase = new Y.Test.Case({
      /*
      * Sets up data needed by each test.
      */
      setUp : function () {
        this.expectedResult = 1.59;
      },
      /*
       * Cleans up everything created by setUp().
       */
      tearDown : function () {
        delete this.expectedResult ;
      },
      testData: function () {
        Y.Assert.areEqual(this.expectedResult,
        convertCurrency(100, 1/63), "100 INR should be equal to
        $ 1.59.");
      }
    });
    //   Using YUI Test console.
    new Y.Test.Console({
      newestOnTop: false,
      width:"400px",
```

```
        height:"300px"
    }).render('#testLogs');

    Y.Test.Runner.add(testCase);
    //run all tests
    Y.Test.Runner.run();
  });
</script>
```

We created a data object, which holds an array in `setUp()` and deletes the object in `tearDown()` to free up memory used. Please note that `setUp()` and `tearDown()` are for data manipulation, and actions or assertions should not be used in these functions. Actual implementations and usage would be more complex, but follow the same process. We created an array, but any kind of value can be assigned as per the requirements.

Test suites

For a project, there would be a number of tests and most of them can be classified in some ways. For example, if a shopping cart is built, there can be tests related to listing of items, items in cart, payments, and so on. In this case, test suites help to organize the tests in groups.

We can use `Y.Test.Suite()` constructor to create a test suite. We can, later, add test cases to the suite and run the suite using `Y.Test.Runner.add(suite)` just like we used to run test cases. Take a look at the following code:

```
<script>
YUI().use('test-console','test', function (Y) {
    //create the test suite
    var suite = new Y.Test.Suite("Testsuite1");

    var testCase = new Y.Test.Case({
      setUp : function () {
        this.expectedResult = 1.59;
      },
      tearDown : function () {
        delete this.expectedResult;
      },

      testData: function () {
        Y.Assert.areEqual(this.expectedResult,
        convertCurrency(100, 1/63), "100 INR should be equal to
        $ 1.59.");
      }
```

```
    });

    //   Using YUI Test console.
    new Y.Test.Console({
      newestOnTop: false,
      width:"400px",
      height:"300px"
    }).render('#testLogs');

    suite.add(testCase);

    Y.Test.Runner.add(suite);
    //run all tests
    Y.Test.Runner.run();
  });
</script>
```

We created a suite named `TestSuite1` in the preceding code and added `testCase` to the suite using the `suite.add()` function call. The name `TestSuite1` is for logging purpose and helps us identify which test suite is running.

Downloading the example code

You can download the example code files from your account at `http://www.packtpub.com` for all the Packt Publishing books you have purchased. If you purchased this book elsewhere, you can visit `http://www.packtpub.com/support` and register to have the files e-mailed directly to you.

Actions and assertions

So far, we have seen very simple tests where only one type of assertion was used. In fact, there are a number of ways you can validate the data. Not only validate the data, but also perform some actions. You will learn about assertions and actions one by one in this section.

Actions

TDD talks about automated testing, and when it comes to JavaScript, we often need to mock user-driven events. These events can be mouse movements, clicks, submitting a form, and so on. While testing, our code depends on other objects, modules, functions, or actions to be performed. It's not always possible or easy to make an actual call to the function. A mock can be used for this purpose. It will imitate the behavior of a real function being mocked.

With YUI, we use a `node-event-simulate` module to simulate native events that behave similar to user generated events. Each framework may define events in its own way, but we are going to see some common scenarios with simple examples in this section:

- **Mouse events**: These events are what users can do with a mouse. There are in total seven events—click, double click, mouse up, mouse down, mouse over, mouse out, and mouse move.

- **Key events**: There are three events—key up, key down, and key press.

- **UI events**: UI events are events which help us change the UI using select, change, blur, focus, scroll, and resize.

- **Touch gestures**: Mobile-first sites are emerging a lot and it is essential to create a mobile site to be on the edge. JavaScript testing frameworks support gesture events testing as well. There are mainly two categories of gestures—single-touch and multi-touch gestures. While there can be a number of gestures, here is the list supported by YUI: single touch/tap, double tap, press, move, flick, two finger gestures—pinch and rotate.

Let's look at the following example. This example showcases a click event on a button, which adds a class clicked to the button and also renders test console:

```
<!DOCTYPE html>
<html> <head>
  <meta charset="UTF-8">
  <title>Chapter - 1</title>

  <link rel="stylesheet" type="text/css"
  href="http://yui.yahooapis.com/2.9.0/build/logger/
  assets/skins/sam/logger.css">
  <script src="http://yui.yahooapis.com/3.18.1/build/yui/yui-
  min.js"></script>
  <script>
    YUI().use('test-console', 'node-event-simulate', function (Y) {
      var controller = {
        handleClick: function(event){
          //   Rendering   YUI Test console.
          new Y.Test.Console({
            filters: {
              fail : true,
              pass : true
            },
            newestOnTop: false,
            width:"400px",
```

```
            height:"300px"
        }).render('# testLogs');

        event.target.addClass("clicked");
    }
}
var testCase = new Y.Test.Case({
    name:'Show log console on click',
    setUp: function(){
        // binding the click event to button
        Y.one('.showLog').on('click', controller.handleClick);
    },
    tearDown: function(){
        Y.one('.showLog').detachAll();
    },
    'handleClick() should show the log console on "clicked"
    and add the class "clicked" to the button':function(){
        var button = Y.one('.showLog');
        // Generating click event
        button.simulate('click');
        Y.Assert.isTrue(button.hasClass('clicked'), 'Button
        should show the log console on "clicked" and have a
        class of "clicked"')
    }
});
Y.Test.Runner.add(testCase);
//run all tests
Y.Test.Runner.run();
});
</script>
</head>
<body class="yui3-skin-sam">
    <div id="testLogs">
    </div>
    <input type="button" class="showLog" value="Show Test Log"
    name="show-log">
</body></html>
```

In the code, we have an object named `controller`, which has a `handleClick` function. This function first renders test console and then adds a class clicked to the caller, which is a button in this case. We have given the `showLog` class already to the button. We have also given a name to the test; this will help us identify which test case passed or fail. It's always a good practice to give the test case a readable name.

In `setUp()`, we bind the click event on the button using this class as selector. We are using the `simulate()` function to generate a click event which calls `handleClick`. In case there was an error creating a test console, the button will not have class clicked assigned, and the assertion in next line will fail. Let's run the preceding code:

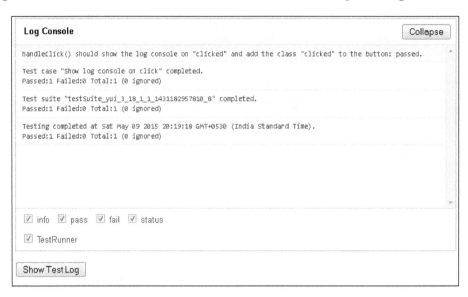

As we can see, the test passed. Class clicked was assigned to button and output of assertion was true. This is how a click event can be generated. Similarly, other events can be generated.

Assertions

Assertions are the key to perform unit tests and validate expression, function, value, state of an object, and so on. A good testing framework has a rich setup assertions. YUI Test has divided assertions into categories. These categories are:

- **Equity assertions**: These are the simplest assertions, which have only two functions `areEqual()` and `areNotEqual()`. Both of these accept three parameters—expected value, actual value, and one optional parameter—error message. The last parameter is used when assertion fails. These assertions use the double equal operator (==) to compare and determine if two values are equal:

```
Y.Assert.areEqual(2, 2);  // Pass
Y.Assert.areEqual(3, "3", "3 was expected"); // Pass
Y.Assert.areNotEqual(2, 4);  // Pass
Y.Assert.areEqual(5, 7, "Five was expected."); // Fail
```

- **Sameness assertions**: There are two assertions in this category: `areSame()` and `areNotSame()`. Similar to equity assertions, these also accept three parameters: expected value, actual value, and one optional parameter—error message. Unlike equity assertions, these functions use triple equals operator (`===`) to determine if values and types of two parameters are similar or not:

```
Y.Assert.areSame(2, 2);   // Pass
Y.Assert.areNotSame(3, "3", "3 was expected"); // Fail
```

- **Data type assertions**: These assertions are useful when you want to check the data type of something before you move to the next step. The data type can be anything such as array, function, Boolean, number, string, and so on. The following are the assertions in this category: `isArray()`, `isBoolean()`, `isFunction()`, `isNumber()`, `isString()`, and `isObject()`. Each of these takes two parameters—the actual value and optional error message.

```
Y.Assert.isString("Test Driven Development Rocks!");   //Pass
Y.Assert.isNumber(23);        //Pass
Y.Assert.isArray([]);         //Pass
Y.Assert.isObject([]);        //Pass
Y.Assert.isFunction(function(){});     //Pass
Y.Assert.isBoolean(true);     //Pass
Y.Assert.isObject(function(){});       //Pass
```

There are two additional assertions in this category for generic purpose, which takes three parameters: expected value, actual value, optional error message. These are `isTypeOf()` and `isInstanceOf()`:

```
Y.Assert.isTypeOf("string", "TDD Rocks");   //Pass
Y.Assert.isTypeOf("number", 23);            //Pass
Y.Assert.isTypeOf("boolean", false);        //Pass
Y.Assert.isTypeOf("object", {});     // Pass
```

- **Special value assertions**: Apart from number, strings, Boolean, there are other value types that also exist in JavaScript. To check those types, there are several assertions available: `isFalse()`, `isTrue()`, `isNaN()`, `isNotNaN()`, `isNull()`, `isNotNull()`, `isUndefined()`, and `isNotUndefined()`. These functions take two parameters: the actual value and optional error message:

```
Y.Assert.isFalse(false);      //Pass
Y.Assert.isTrue(true);        //Pass
Y.Assert.isNaN(NaN);          //Pass
Y.Assert.isNotNaN(23);         //Pass
Y.Assert.isNull(null);        //Pass
Y.Assert.isNotNull(undefined);     //Pass
Y.Assert.isUndefined(undefined);   //Pass
Y.Assert.isNotUndefined(null);     //Pass
```

- **Forced failures**: There are times when you need to create your own assertions or you want an assertion to fail intentionally. In this case, you can use the `fail()` assertion. This assertion takes one optional parameter as an error message:

```
Y.Assert.fail();  // The test will fail here.
Y.Assert.fail("This test should fail.");
```

Similar to YUI, other frameworks do have assertions. Their naming standards may be different, but almost all these assertions are present in major testing frameworks.

Benefits and pitfalls

We have seen how easy it is to create test cases, run them, and analyze the report. Every framework has some benefits and pitfalls. In this section, we will look at some generic benefits and pitfalls.

Benefits of unit testing

The following are a few benefits of using unit testing for our projects:

- **Quickly making big changes**: We can make big changes easily if we have included unit tests in system. As we know, it works properly because we have run the tests, we simply need to make sure that its working now by just running test again.

- **Boost your confidence**: Unit testing helps you to boost up your confidence about requirements completion. It helps you to make a decision about when you can stop coding. Tests give you confidence that you have performed enough coding for one requirement and now we can move to other requirements. If unit tests are written properly and run every time when we carry out minor changes, then we can easily catch any bugs introduced due to change.

- **Helps to understand system design**: Unit tests help you to understand system design and code written by developers. Instead of spending time to understand code, you can focus on outlining conditions and boundaries for the code and output that we expect from that. Good unit tests can help document and define what something is supposed to do.

- **Green lighting development**: When we see green light at a traffic signal, the same feeling we get once we see successful output from any unit test. Likewise, we can even get the point from where we left by seeing the next red signal on the way which needs fixing. This way, we can easily get feedback for our code and visual effect for the same.

- **Faster development**: Some people have a belief that writing unit tests double the effort to complete any development or take more time to complete any module, but unlikely that belief is not right. Writing unit test is relatively less tough and takes less effort and save more time in completing the development for any system. One can realize this by including unit test in their system.

- **Easy debugging**: Let's say we wrote some code, there are some errors reported and we need to fix them. We will check in my browser for the issue, using a developer tool like Firebug. We will try to check for JavaScript errors via console log. After understanding the issue, we will make some changes, go back to browser, reload the page, and check if the error still exists. We would even need to make some changes to DOM via command line or debug via script tab. But if we had unit tests, we would have run the tests and see all the issues at once. One more advantage can be considered in case of unit test is whenever any test fails; only latest changes need to be checked/debugged. We don't need to check the whole module again.

- **Reusable code**: In order to write unit test for any system, we need to make code modular. This simply means that we can easily reuse and understand that code in near future. This way, we increase production of reusable code in the system.

- **Saving cost**: By writing a unit test, we will save cost for any system as we will find more defects in the development phase in comparison to acceptance testing phase or go live phase. That way we are saving time, effort, and cost.

Pitfalls of unit testing

We have seen different benefits of unit testing; now let's see what kind of pitfalls can occur during unit testing implementation:

- **Wrong assumptions for unit testing**: Unit testing is not a tool, it's a methodology or technique. We need a set of acquired skills to understand that methodology. Sometimes, we do correct coding, but with wrong assumptions and it can happen that we end up writing wrong unit test. This can happen to anybody. It needs proper training and experience. Before writing any unit test, it is necessary that we understand the method of writing unit test. Only then we implement that in our system.

- **Not suitable when under tight deadlines**: Many times it happens that deadlines for development are very tight or strict. In that case, it will be difficult for any developer to allot proper time for writing unit test. It is normally the job of the whole organization to understand the importance of unit test and give proper timing to develop good quality unit test.

Summary

So far, we have seen how to write simple unit tests, advance them using some actions and assertions. This chapter showcased tests, actions, and assertions using YUI. YUI is used to give an idea of how all this happens and works together through the TDD life cycle. Then you learned about some benefits and pitfalls.

In the next chapter, you will learn about popular JavaScript tools and frameworks. YUI was a browser-based testing framework, but later we will also check tools, which don't need you to run test cases in the browser.

3
Testing Tools

There are so many tools and frameworks available in the market to perform unit testing for any logical JavaScript code. It's necessary that we understand the way these tools work, since it's important to identify a good fit for a project. Though it's not possible to explain all the tools in one chapter or a book, yet some popular tools are included in this chapter. We can write tests with the usage of some test framework and just run them in the browser, on some static page. But for automation, when we use Jenkins (or other tools for continuous integration), we need some tool that can run our tests automatically such as Karma, PhantomJS, and many more. Each of these tools are explained in three subtopics like setup, writing tests, and running tests.

We will be covering the following testing frameworks and tools in this chapter:

- JsUnit
- QUnit
- Karma with Jasmine
- DalekJS

JsUnit

JsUnit is an open source unit testing framework created by Edward Hieat. It is basically used to perform unit testing for client side in browser testing. JsUnit comes with ant tasks, which can be helpful to integrate it with continuous integration server builds.

Getting started

Download the ZIP bundle of JsUnit from `http://sourceforge.net/projects/` `jsunit/files/` or `https://github.com/pivotal/jsunit` location. Extract ZIP file in any directory, and you will get the `jsunit` directory. In this book, we will be using `jsunit v2.2` for example. Once you extract the ZIP file, you will get the folder structure shown in the following screenshot:

Name	Date modified	Type	Size
app	5/16/2015 2:56 PM	File folder	
bin	5/16/2015 2:56 PM	File folder	
css	5/16/2015 2:56 PM	File folder	
doc	5/16/2015 2:56 PM	File folder	
images	5/16/2015 2:56 PM	File folder	
java	5/16/2015 2:56 PM	File folder	
lib	5/16/2015 2:56 PM	File folder	
licenses	5/16/2015 2:56 PM	File folder	
tests	5/16/2015 2:56 PM	File folder	
build.xml	11/25/2009 7:31 AM	XML File	9 KB
build_aggregate.xml	11/25/2009 7:31 AM	XML File	6 KB
jsCurrencyConversionTests.html	5/19/2015 6:32 PM	Firefox HTML Doc...	1 KB
jsunit.properties.sample	11/25/2009 7:31 AM	SAMPLE File	4 KB
jsUnitTestSuite.html	5/19/2015 6:36 PM	Firefox HTML Doc...	1 KB
logging.properties	11/25/2009 7:31 AM	PROPERTIES File	1 KB
readme.txt	11/25/2009 7:31 AM	Text Document	1 KB
testRunner.html	11/25/2009 7:31 AM	Firefox HTML Doc...	3 KB

This folder structure contains example tests for JsUnit in the `tests` folder. If we want to start test suite to run the test that we have written, then we need to click on the file called `testRunner.html`. Once we click on test runner, we can see screen as shown in the following screenshot:

We can give our test file path in the **file:///** field as shown in preceding image and then click on **Run** to see the status of tests that we have written. We will understand more about this in the next subsection.

Writing tests

Until now, we understood basic things about JsUnit; now, let's see how to write test using JsUnit and understand the features available in the framework:

- **Test pages and test functions**: Test page in JsUnit contains an HTML page with test functions in it. Test function can be distinguished with prefix test in function from other function in the page—it must begin with `test`. Apart from this, the test function does not contain any parameters. Its signature can be like `testCurrencyConversion()`.

  To run the test, we need to include `app/jsUnitCore.js` in our HTML file. `jsUnitCore.js` is the test engine for our application. JsUnit will discover test function from the test page as we are following naming convention with prefix `test` in each and every test function.

- **Assertions functions,** `setUp()`**, and** `tearDown()`: JsUnit contains the following assertions that we can use for our test cases:

    ○   `assert([comment], booleanValue)`

    ○   `assertTrue([comment], booleanValue)`

    ○   `assertFalse([comment], booleanValue)`

    ○   `assertEquals([comment], value1, value2)`

    ○   `assertNotEquals([comment], value1, value2)`

    ○   `assertNull([comment], value)`

    ○   `assertNotNull([comment], value)`

    ○   `assertUndefined([comment], value)`

    ○   `assertNotUndefined([comment], value)`

    ○   `assertNaN([comment], value)`

    ○   `assertNotNaN([comment], value)`

    ○   `fail(comment)`

    In each assertion, the `comment` argument is optional. Along with assertions, JsUnit has the `JSUNIT_UNDEFINED_VALUE` variable which is a JavaScript undefined value. We have seen use of `setUp()` and `tearDown()` in *Chapter 2, Testing Concepts,* in detail. Similarly, we can use the `setUp()` and `tearDown()` functions in JsUnit.

- **Test suites**: Test suite in JsUnit is set of test pages. Common use of the test suite page is to group all test pages in one page. We can define the test suite function in JsUnit with the use of the `suite()` function. We can add test pages with the use of the `addTestPage()` function in the test suite file, where the filename parameter is fully qualified or a relative URL of file. We can add test suite with the use of the `addTestSuite()` function. Test suite can only be added with the use of `addTestSuite()`, if we have added suite with the `suite()` function in the same file.

- **Tracing/logging**: Normally, we debug JavaScript with the use of the `alert()` function, firebug like browser plugins, and so on. In JsUnit, we have three levels of tracing available to debug JavaScript—warn, info, and debug.

    Whenever we run our test in test runner, we can set the tracing level. If we set warn, then we can see all warn traces. If we set info, then we can see warn and info traces. If we set debug, we can see all traces. The following are the syntaxes for writing traces in JsUnit:

    ○   `function warn(message, [value])`

- ° function inform(message, [value]) (equivalent to function info(message, [value]))
- ° function debug(message, [value])

Running tests

So far, we have seen that all the options that are available to write tests in JsUnit. Now we will see how we can run an example test in JsUnit.

We will convert our currency conversion example in the JsUnit framework that we have written in *Chapter 2, Testing Concepts*, with the use of the YUI Tests framework. We have seen option to add test pages in the preceding sections called *Writing tests*. In our example, we will first write our currency conversion page as follows:

```html
<!DOCTYPE html>
<html>
<head>
    <meta charset="UTF-8">
    <title>Chapter - 3</title>

    <!-- Source file -->
    <script src="app/jsUnitCore.js"></script>

    <script>
        function testConvertCurrency(amount, rateOfConversion){
            var toCurrencyAmount = 0;
            // conversion
            toCurrencyAmount = rateOfConversion * amount;
            // rounding off
            toCurrencyAmount = parseFloat(toCurrencyAmount).toFixed(2);
            return toCurrencyAmount;
        }
        function testData() {
            assertEquals("Assert
            passed",'1.59',testConvertCurrency(100,1/63));
        }
        function testData1() {
            assertNotEquals("Assert
            Failed",'2.00',testConvertCurrency(100,1/63));
        }
    </script>
```

```
    </head>
    <body>
    <h1>JsUnit Currency Conversion Tests</h1>

    <p>This page contains tests for the JsUnit currency conversion. To
    see them, take a look at the source.</p>
    </body>
    </html>
```

In the mentioned example, we have declared a function called the testConvertCurrency function. In the preceding section, we have already seen that to write any test function, we need to add the test prefix. In next two functions, we have written two asserts to test our currency convert logic that we have written. Let's see how we can add this test page into the test suite:

```
    <!DOCTYPE html>
    <html>
    <head>
        <meta charset="UTF-8">
        <title>Chapter - 3</title>

        <!-- Source file -->
        <script src="app/jsUnitCore.js"></script>

        <script>
            function coreSuite() {
                var result = new JsUnitTestSuite();
                result.addTestPage("jsCurrencyConversionTests.html");
                return result;
            }
            function suite() {
                var newsuite = new JsUnitTestSuite();
                newsuite.addTestSuite(coreSuite());
                return newsuite;
            }
        </script>

    </head>
    <body>
    <h1>JsUnit Test Suite</h1>

    <p>This page contains a suite of tests for testing JsUnit.</p>
    </body>
    </html>
```

In the preceding code, we have two functions: coreSuite() and suite(). In coreSuite(), we are adding test page, and in suite() function, we are adding our test suite for our test runner.

We will now see how this test suite looks when we run it in the test runner:

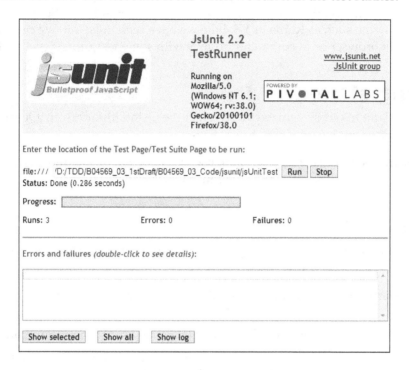

In the preceding screenshot, we can see that our one test ran successfully and one test failed as we have passed wrong output in our one of assert. If you click on the filename in the errors section, then it will show details about the error and message that we have set in our code.

So far, we have seen that how can we write test using JsUnit with the use of actions, assertions, and test suites. We also used runner in which we can give a test file and run the test by clicking on the **Run** button.

QUnit

QUnit is JavaScript test framework, which can be used to run unit test written in JavaScript. QUnit is used by jQuery, jQuery UI, and jQuery mobile projects. QUnit was originally developed by John Resig as a part of jQuery. QUnit is normally used to test the JavaScript code and it's even used to test server-side JavaScript via some JavaScript engine such as Rhine or V8. Like we have seen in JsUnit, we can run the QUnit test in browser or in command prompt with some test runner such as Karma.

Getting started

To install QUnit in our system, we need to get the QUnit library from jQuery CDN (`http://code.jquery.com/qunit/`).

Two files are needed to run test with the use of QUnit: `qunit.js` and `quint.css`. Once we download these files, then we can start writing our tests.

Writing tests

Let's see how we can write test using QUnit and know about assertions available in QUnit:

- **Assertions**: QUnit contains the following assertions that we can use to write any test:
    - `async()`: Instruct QUnit to wait for an asynchronous operation
    - `equal(actual, expected, message)`: A non-strict comparison, roughly equivalent to JUnit's `assertEquals`
    - `expect(asserts)`: Specify how many assertions are expected to run within a test
    - `notEqual(actual, expected, message)`: A non-strict comparison, checking for inequality
    - `deepEqual(actual, expected, message)`: A deep recursive comparison, working on primitive types, arrays, objects, regular expressions, dates, and functions
    - `notDeepEqual(actual, expected, message)`: An inverted deep recursive comparison, working on primitive types, arrays, objects, regular expressions, dates, and functions
    - `ok(result, message)`: A Boolean check, equivalent to CommonJS's `assert.ok()` and JUnit's `assertTrue()`. Passes if the first argument is `truthy`

- ◦ `notOk(result, message)`: A Boolean check, inverse of ok() and CommonJS's assert.ok(), and equivalent to JUnit's assertFalse(). Passes if the first argument is `falsy`

- ◦ `strictEqual(actual, expected, message)`: A strict type and value comparison

- ◦ `notStrictEqual(actual, expected, message)`: A strict comparison, checking for inequality

- ◦ `propEqual(actual, expected, message)`: A strict type and value comparison of an object's own properties

- ◦ `notPropEqual(actual, expected, message)`: A strict comparison of an object's own properties, checking for inequality

- ◦ `push()`: Report the result of a custom assertion

- ◦ `throws()`: Test if a callback throws an exception, and optionally compare the thrown error

- **Callbacks**: When integrating QUnit into other tools such as CI servers, use these callbacks as an API to read the test results:

  - ◦ `QUnit.begin()`: Register a callback to fire whenever the test suite begins

  - ◦ `QUnit.done()`: Register a callback to fire whenever the test suite ends

  - ◦ `QUnit.log()`: Register a callback to fire whenever an assertion completes

  - ◦ `QUnit.moduleDone()`: Register a callback to fire whenever a module ends

  - ◦ `QUnit.moduleStart()`: Register a callback to fire whenever a module begins

  - ◦ `QUnit.testDone()`: Register a callback to fire whenever a test ends

  - ◦ `QUnit.testStart()`: Register a callback to fire whenever a test begins

- **Test**: Functions that are available to write test in QUnit are listed as follows:

  - ◦ `QUnit.module()`: Group-related tests under a single label

  - ◦ `QUnit.skip()`: Adds a test like object to be skipped

  - ◦ `QUnit.test()`: Add a test to run

Running tests

Let's run our currency conversion example in QUnit. To write that example in QUnit, we need to first write our currency conversion function in `currencyConversionTest.js`, as shown in the following snippet:

```
var convertINR ={
    currencyConversion : function(amount, rateOfConversion){
        var toCurrencyAmount = 0;
        // conversion
        toCurrencyAmount = rateOfConversion * amount;
        // rounding off
        toCurrencyAmount = parseFloat(toCurrencyAmount).toFixed(2);
        return toCurrencyAmount;
    }
}
```

Now let's write test for our currency conversion function in `unitTest.js` as shown in the following snippet. In this snippet, we used assertions and test function of QUnit to test currency conversion functionality:

```
QUnit.test("currency conversion example", function( assert ) {
    assert.equal(convertINR.currencyConversion(100,1/63),'1.59',
    "100 INR is equal to 1.59 USD" );
});
```

Now we will write the test suite HTML file `testSuite.html` as shown in the following snippets. Here in this file, we included all modules:

```
<!DOCTYPE html>
<html>
<head>
  <meta charset="utf-8">
  <title>QUnit basic example</title>
  <link rel="stylesheet" href="qunit-1.18.0.css">
</head>
<body>
  <div id="qunit"></div>
  <div id="qunit-fixture"></div>
  <script src="qunit-1.18.0.js"></script>
  <script src="unitTests.js"></script>
  <script src="currencyConversionTest.js"></script>
</body>
</html>
```

Let's see what happens when we run the test in browser in the following screenshot:

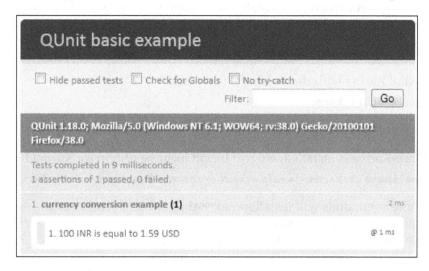

As we have seen, we only needed two files `qunit.js` and `qunit.css` to perform testing using Qunit. As the names suggest, JS file provides framework, which we can use to write test. To show our results with proper UI, we need to include the CSS file.

Karma with Jasmine

Karma is a JavaScript command line tool that can be used to open a browser, which loads an application's source code and executes tests. Karma can be configured to run against a number of browsers, which is useful to boost any developers confident that the application works on all browsers that we need to support. Normally, Karma tests are executed on the command prompt and it will display the results of unit tests on the command prompt once a test is run in the browser.

Getting started

Karma runs on Node.js and it is available as a NPM package. To perform a setup of Karma, we first need Node.js installed in our machine. Let's first install Node.js on the machine. To install Node.js, we need to download it from `http://blog.nodejs.org/2014/06/16/node-v0-10-29-stable/`. Currently, Karma supports three stable versions of Node.js, which is 0.8.x, 0.10.x, and 0.12.x. We will install 0.10.29 Version for this chapter.

Once we installed Node.js, we can install Karma plugins with the use of command prompt. The best approach is to install Karma locally in our project directory. Open project path in command prompt and then use the following commands.

Let's see how we can carry out setup for Karma in the following steps:

1. Install Karma with the use of the command:

   ```
   npm install karma -save-dev
   ```

   This command will install Karma with Version 0.12.32

2. Once Karma is installed, we will install Jasmine plugin for Karma here:

   ```
   npm install karma-jasmine karma-chrome-launcher -save-dev
   ```

   These commands will install `karma`, `karma-jasmine`, and `karma-chrome-launcher` packages into `node_modules` in your `project` directory. We can use many test frameworks with Karma, such as `karma-jasmine`, `karma-quint`, and many more. However here, we are using `karma-jasmine` to demonstrate examples. It will save development dependencies into `package.json` so that any other developer working on the project needs to run `npm install` in order to get dependencies installed.

3. We will install Karma globally with the use of `cli` plugin so that we can start Karma from anywhere:

   ```
   npm install -g karma-cli
   ```

4. Now we can start Karma from anywhere. But to start with, we first need to initialize Karma configuration file.

   ```
   karma init karma.conf.js
   ```

5. Once we initialize configuration file, then we can start Karma with the use of the following command. This command will show results of test that we have written:

   ```
   karma start karma.conf.js
   ```

Writing tests

Here, we are using Jasmine with Karma, so let's see how we can write test using Jasmine in Karma. You will learn more about Jasmine in the next chapter.

- The `describe` function: We can define different specifications together with the use of the `describe` function blocks:

  ```
  describe("A Specification Suite",function(){
  …..
  });
  ```

- The `it` and `expect` function: Specifications are expressed with the use of the `it` function. Expectations can be expressed using the `expect` function:

```
describe("A Specification Suite",function(){
    it("contains spec with an explanation", function(){
        expect(view.tagName).toBe('div');
    });
});
```

Matchers can be used to get Boolean comparison between the actual value and expected value. Normally, it reports expectation as true of false to Jasmine. Let's see some matchers that we can use in Jasmine, we explained the same in more detail in *Chapter 4, Jasmine*.

- `not`
- `toBe`
- `toEqual`
- `toMatch`
- `toBeDefined`
- `toBeUndefined`
- `toBeNull`
- `toBeTruthy`
- `toBeFalsy`
- `toContain`
- `toBeLessThan`
- `toBeGreaterThan`
- `toBeCloseTo`
- `toThrow`

- `beforeEach`: In Jasmine, to set up a test, the `beforeEach()` function is used:

```
describe("EveryDay.ToDoList",function(){
    var list;
    beforeEach(function(){
        list = new EveryDay.ToDoList();
    });
    it("sets to tagName to 'div'",function(){
        expect(view.tagName).toBe('div');
    });
});
```

- afterEach: In Jasmine, to tear down a test, the afterEach() function is used:

```
describe("EveryDay.ToDoList",function(){
    var list;
    beforeEach(function(){
        list = new EveryDay.ToDoList();
    });
    afterEach(function(){
        list = null;
    });
    It("sets to tagName to 'div'",function(){
        expect(view.tagName).toBe('div');
    });
});
```

- **Custom matchers**: Let's see how we can define custom matchers in Jasmine:

```
beforeEach(function(){
    this.addMatchers({
        toBeGreaterThan: function(expected){
            var actual = this.actual;
            …..
            this.message = function(){
                return "message"
            }
            return actual > expected;
        }
    });
});
```

- **Asynchronous support**: It includes the runs and waitsFor blocks and a latch function. The latch function polls until it returns true or the timeout expires, whichever comes first.

  If the timeout expires, the specifications fails with a message:

```
runs(functionname);
waitsfor(function(), {
    return;
});
```

Running tests

To run any test with the use of Karma, we first need to write our require JS file and put it in the `js` folder. We will convert our currency conversion example. Create the `currency-conversion.js` file in the `js` folder using the following code:

```
function convertCurrency(amount,rateOfConversion)
{
    var toCurrencyAmount = 0;
    // conversion
    toCurrencyAmount = rateOfConversion * amount;
    // rounding off
    toCurrencyAmount = parseFloat(toCurrencyAmount).toFixed(2);
    return toCurrencyAmount;
}
```

Then write your test in the `test` folder. Create the `unit-test.js` file and put the following code in it:

```
describe('Convert Currency', function() {
    it('100 INR should be equal to $ 1.59', function() {
        expect(convertCurrency(100, 1/63)).toEqual('1.59');
    });
});
```

Once we are done with writing our `unit-test.js` file, we need to include this entire configuration in the `karma.conf.js` file. Open configuration file and then modify the following lines:

```
// list of files / patterns to load in the browser
    files: ['js/currency-convertor.js',
        'test/*.js'
    ],
```

Once we add file and test it in the configuration file, then we can do other settings in configuration files like `autoWatch:true`. It will allow us to watch the file and execute the test whenever any file changes. Other option that we can change is `singleRun:true`, which can help Karma capture browsers, run the tests, and then exit.

In the previous example, we have seen how can we add files in the configuration files. Let's see how we can exclude file from the setup with the following example:

```
//list of files / patterns to exclude from test
exclude: ['js/abc.js',
        abc/*.js'
        ],
```

We can run our test now with the use of command that we have seen earlier.

```
Karma start karma.conf.js
```

It will run our test in the browser and then close the browser. It will show our test result in command line as shown in the following figure:

```
C:\Users\hetal.prajapati>karma start karma.conf.js
INFO [karma]: Karma v0.12.32 server started at http://localhost:9876/
INFO [launcher]: Starting browser Chrome
INFO [Chrome 43.0.2357 (Windows 7)]: Connected on socket 19An-PRtEDhSX9SWAAAA with id 14993113
Chrome 43.0.2357 (Windows 7): Executed 1 of 1 SUCCESS (0.023 secs / 0.004 secs)

C:\Users\hetal.prajapati>
```

If any test fails to run, then it will show the result as shown in the following screenshot:

```
C:\Users\hetal.prajapati>karma start karma.conf.js
INFO [karma]: Karma v0.12.32 server started at http://localhost:9876/
INFO [launcher]: Starting browser Chrome
INFO [Chrome 43.0.2357 (Windows 7)]: Connected on socket 36fPju9oQgK5L1XDAAAA with id 22811
629
Chrome 43.0.2357 (Windows 7) Convert Currency 100 INR should be equal to $ 1.59 FAILED
        Expected '1.59' to equal '0.09'.
            at Object.<anonymous> (C:/Users/hetal.prajapati/test/unit-test.js:3:38)
Chrome 43.0.2357 (Windows 7): Executed 1 of 1 (1 FAILED) ERROR (0.034 secs / 0.013 secs)

C:\Users\hetal.prajapati>
```

Karma is just a tool which needs any framework to be included to perform testing in Karma. We used Jasmine here. Karma has plugins for testing frameworks (such as Jasmine, Mocha, and QUnit). You can check the source code of the existing plugins and write your own plugin for the desired testing framework.

DalekJS

DalekJS provides simple and fast way to do automated web testing. It supports almost all kinds of browsers and can script them, takes screenshots, and creates reports about the tests. DalekJS is an open source tool, which can be used to perform UI testing written in JavaScript. It will be used to launch and automate the users' browser, fill values automatically and submit the forms, click on elements and links on the page, capture screenshots, and run the tests which have been written to test functional use cases.

Getting started

In this section, you will learn about DalekJS. It is an automated browser testing tool with JavaScript. With DalekJS, we can even run tests directly in Firefox, Google Chrome, or Internet Explorer.

Create a `package.json` file in your work directory:

```
Package.json:
{
  "name": "myCssTardis", // Name of your project
  "description": "Is awesome",//Description
  "version": "0.0.2"  //version of DalekJS
}
```

First install Node.js into your system. To install Node.js, we need to download it from `http://blog.nodejs.org/2014/06/16/node-v0-10-29-stable/`.

DalekJS works on the two latest stable versions, that is, 0.8.x and 0.10.x at this point.

Install DalekJS using the npm command as follows:

```
npm install dalek-cli -g
npm install dalekjs --save-dev
```

For this chapter the following versions are installed using the preceding commands:

```
DalekJS CLI Tools Version: 0.0.5
DalekJS  local install: 0.0.9
```

Write your first test as shown in the following code snippet:

```
module.exports = {
'Page title is as per expectation': function (test) {
  test
    .open('http://google.com')
    .assert.title().is('Google', 'Title exists')
    .done();
}
};
```

Let's see what we are getting on command prompt when we run our first test in the following screenshot:

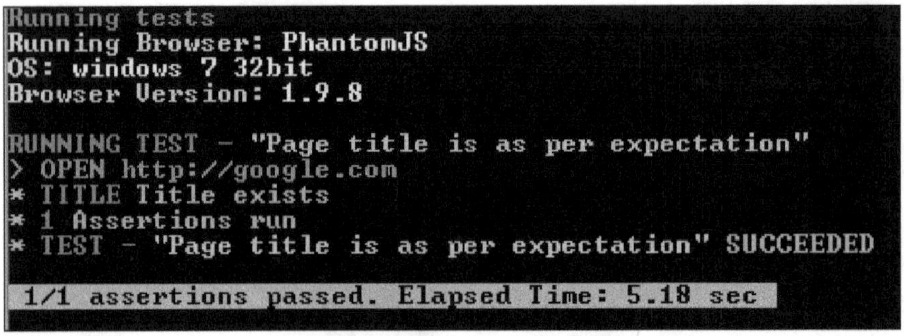

```
Running tests
Running Browser: PhantomJS
OS: windows 7 32bit
Browser Version: 1.9.8

RUNNING TEST - "Page title is as per expectation"
> OPEN http://google.com
* TITLE Title exists
* 1 Assertions run
* TEST - "Page title is as per expectation" SUCCEEDED

1/1 assertions passed. Elapsed Time: 5.18 sec
```

Add a "real" browser using the following command:

```
npm install dalek-browser-chrome --save-dev
```

Run your test again using the following command:

```
dalek test/firstTest.js -b chrome
```

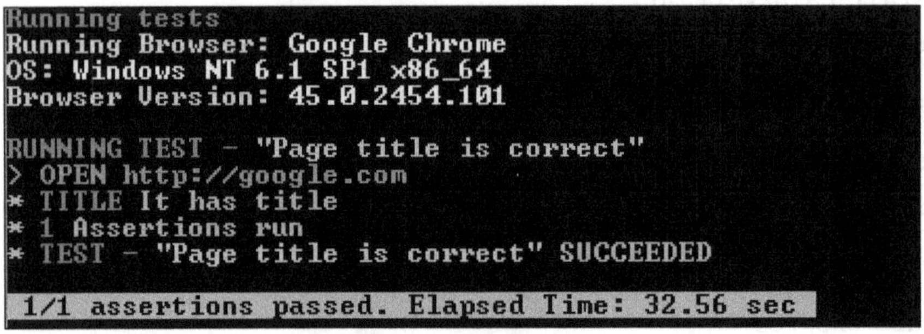

```
Running tests
Running Browser: Google Chrome
OS: Windows NT 6.1 SP1 x86_64
Browser Version: 45.0.2454.101

RUNNING TEST - "Page title is correct"
> OPEN http://google.com
* TITLE It has title
* 1 Assertions run
* TEST - "Page title is correct" SUCCEEDED

1/1 assertions passed. Elapsed Time: 32.56 sec
```

We will now create an HTML report of your test. We need to install the HTML reporter to create and view reports. To install reporter, we can use the following command:

```
npm install dalek-reporter-html --save-dev
```

Writing tests

Now when we have everything ready, we will see how to write a test in DalekJS with the use of actions and assertions.

Actions

Actions can be used to control browsers. For example, simulate user interactions such as clicking elements, open popups, and so on.

- `.query`: Sometimes it will be cumbersome to write the same selector again and again. Instead of writing the selector tag again, we can use `.query`.

- `.toWindow`: When we want to switch to some other context like a popup window then we can use `.toWindow`.

- `toParentWindow`: It will switch back to the parent context when the test context has been switched to some other window context.

- `.screenshot`: It will take a screenshot of the current page or CSS element.

- `.wait`: It will pause the test suite execution for some amount of time and optionally execute a step on done.

- `.click`: It will click on a particular element that has been given with selector in the method.

- `.submit`: It will submit a form.

- `.open`: It will be used to open HTTP request for opening a given location. We can use GET, POST, PUT, DELETE, and HEAD requests.

- `.type`: It will type a text in the textarea or textbox. We can even send special keys using Unicode characters.

- `.execute`: It will execute a JavaScript from the browser. We can also pass parameters to JavaScript function.

- `.accept`: It will accept an alert/prompt/confirm dialog. This can be basically same clicking on **OK** in alert or **Yes**/**No** in the confirmation dialog.

- `.resize`: It will resize a browser width to get to a set of dimensions given. The default value is 1280 px width and 1024 px height. We can even specify our default value in the configuration.

- `.setCookie`: It will set a cookie with a specific name and content.

- `.setValue`: It will set a value in the form fields with given values.

- `.log.message`: It will display user-defined log messages.

- `.close`: It will close an active window and automatically select a parent window.

There are many other actions available, which we can use. We also included few actions, which are more important.

Assertions

The following are the assertions available for DalekJS:

- `.chain`: It will be cumbersome to write assert in each and every statement, so instead of writing assert again and again, we can use the `.chain` assert

- `.end`: It will terminate an assert chain or a query

- `.width`: It will check the actual width of an element

- `.height`: It will check the actual height of an element

- `.exists`: It will verify that an element matching the provided selector expression exists in the remote dom environment

- `.doesntExist`: It will verify that an element matching the provided selector expression not exists in the remote dom environment

- `.attr`: It will assert that element attributes are as per the expectation

- `.url`: It will assert that the page's URL is as per expectation

- `.dialogText`: It will assert that the given text exists in the provided alert/confirm dialog

- `.title`: It will assert that the page title is as per expectation

There are many other assertions available that we can use. We included a few important assertions only.

Running tests

Let's run our currency conversion example into the DalekJS framework. Create `index.html` with use of the following code:

```
<!DOCTYPE html>
<html>
<head>
  <meta charset="UTF-8">
  <title>Chapter 3 - DalekJS</title>
</head>
<script>
    function convertCurrency(amount, rateOfConversion) {

        var toCurrencyAmount = 0;
```

```
        // conversion
        toCurrencyAmount = 1/rateOfConversion * amount;

        // rounding off
        toCurrencyAmount =
        parseFloat(toCurrencyAmount).toFixed(2);

        document.getElementById('toCurrencyAmount').value =
        '$'+toCurrencyAmount;
    }
</script>
<body>
    <input id="amount" name="amount" type="text" value="" />

    <input id="rateOfConversion" name="rateOfConversion"
    type="text" value="" />

    <input id="convert" name="convert" type="submit"
    value="Convert" onClick="convertCurrency
    (document.getElementById('amount')
    .value,document.getElementById('rateOfConversion').value)" />

    <input id="toCurrencyAmount" name="toCurrencyAmount"
    type="text" value="" />

</body>
</html>
```

Now add `test.js` with the following content:

```
module.exports = {
  'Testing convertCurrency': function (test) {
    var actualResult = '1.59'
    test
    .open('index.html')
      .type('#amount', '100')
      .type('#rateOfConversion', '63')
      .click('#convert')
      .assert.val('#toCurrencyAmount', '$1.59')
      .screenshot('test2.png')
    .done();
  }
};
```

Run test with the use of the `dalek test.js` command, and you will see the following output in the command shell:

```
Running tests
Running Browser: PhantomJS
OS: windows 7 32bit
Browser Version: 1.9.8

RUNNING TEST - "Testing convertCurrency"
> OPEN index.html
> TYPE #amount
> TYPE #rateOfConversion
> CLICK #convert
* VAL
> SCREENSHOT test2.png
* 1 Assertions run
* TEST - "Testing convertCurrency" SUCCEEDED

1/1 assertions passed. Elapsed Time: 2.05 sec
```

In the preceding code snippet, we added the `.screenshot('test2.png')` command to take a screenshot of the browser to run the code that we have written. We will get the following screenshot:

| 100 | 63 | Convert | $1.59 |

Similar to Karma, we have to install DalekJS on the `Node.js` framework. DalekJS is a fully open source and invented to fulfill some specific project needs. Creators of DalekJS says, "DalekJS was born in battle, full of blood and anger, and therefore is buggy as hell and not ready for production yet". You should always check all open bugs before using it for your project.

Summary

In this chapter, we have seen how to write unit tests with the use of different tools such as JsUnit, QUnit, Karma, and DalekJS. You learned how can you install different tools, use them to write different tests, and finally wrote one example in each and every tool to understand them in detail.

In fact, there are so many tools available, sometimes created eventually to satisfy specific requirements, or as an improvement to some existing tool or framework. The purpose of this chapter was to showcase a variety and a couple of different syntax these tools use. The point to mention here is that despite the difference in syntax or naming conventions, almost all of the tools use assertions, actions, suits, set up, tear down, and so on.

In the next chapter, you will learn about Jasmine in more detail and understand how Jasmine works with the use of some examples.

4
Jasmine

The previous chapter introduced a number of JavaScript tools and frameworks, Jasmine was one of them. This chapter will showcase more about Jasmine. Jasmine is known as a behavior-driven development framework, popularly used for unit testing of JavaScript code, which makes it essential to read and understand the differences between test-driven and behavior-driven development.

We are going to learn the following:

- Understanding behavior-driven development
- Jasmine framework
- Advantages and disadvantages

Understanding behavior-driven development

A very important thing to learn about TDD is that it's not about just testing, but it's more than that. It defines a process and encourages to improve the overall design of a system. We have seen in *Chapter 1*, *Overview of TDD*, and *Chapter 2*, *Testing Concepts*, that tests written in TDD not only test our projects, but they also act as documentation and are useful in many more ways. But most of the developers tend to take it just for testing and are not able to harness the benefit of TDD beyond that; probably, because the title mentions *test* in TDD.

Behavior-driven development (BDD) is a term introduced by Dan North to address this shortcoming. The terminology used by BDD focuses on the behavioral aspect of the system. In this chapter, you are going to learn about Jasmine in detail and note that the differences in nomenclature of TDD and BDD. Deep down, TDD and BDD would serve the same purpose, but using the vocabulary of BDD gives you a better set of tests and documents your system in a better way.

While TDD interface gives names such as `suite()`, `test()`, `setup()`, `teardown()`, `suiteSetup()`, `suiteTearDown()`, `assert()`, and so on. BDD offers `describe()`, `context()`, `it()`, `beforeEach()`, `afterEach()`, `beforeAll()`, `afterAll()`, `expect()`, and so on. A test suite in TDD is usually created using `suite()`, while BDD uses `describe()`; to create a unit test TDD uses `test()` and BDD uses `it()`. Follow the table here for the differences:

Description	What TDD uses	What BDD uses
Test suite	`suite()`	`describe()`
Unit test	`test()`	`it()`
Actions before a test runs	`setup()`	`beforeEach()`
Actions after a test runs	`teardown()`	`afterEach()`
Actions before a suite runs	`suiteSetup()`	`beforeAll()`
Actions after a suite runs	`suiteTearDown()`	`afterAll()`
Assertions	`assert()`	`expect()`

Setting up Jasmine

Jasmine does not depend on any other JavaScript frameworks. It is available as a standalone release at `https://github.com/jasmine/jasmine/releases`. We are going to pick a stable version, for example, v2.3.0 for this chapter. We can download a ZIP file of standalone release, which we need to extract and use. After extraction, the folder structure looks like this:

Name	Date modified	Type	Size
lib	6/9/2015 7:27 AM	File folder	
spec	6/9/2015 7:27 AM	File folder	
src	6/9/2015 7:27 AM	File folder	
MIT.LICENSE	4/28/2015 9:59 AM	LICENSE File	2 KB
SpecRunner.html	4/28/2015 9:59 AM	Firefox HTML...	1 KB

In the `lib` folder, we require the CSS and JS files to be included.

We have seen test runners for many tools so far, Jasmine has `SpecRunner`. We will see how it looks later in this chapter when we will run our tests.

describe and specs

We have seen tests suites in many tools in the previous chapters. In Jasmine, we use describe to start a test suite. describe is a global function, which takes two parameters—a string and a function. The string is the title for the suite and function contains all of the tests implementations. A test in Jasmine is known as **spec**. The parameter function in the describe function contains one or more specs. A spec is also defined by calling a global function it, which takes two parameters just like describe.

Let's take a look at the following code:

```
describe("Title of a Suite", function() {
// variables available for all specs
    var amountToConvert;
    var rateOfConversion;

// the function 'it' defines a spec
    it("Title of a Spec", function() {
       // do some testing here
    });
    it("Another spec", function() {
       // do some testing here
          });
});
```

As seen from the preceding code, describe defined a suite and specs were defined using it. To make these functions available, we need to use Jasmine JavaScript libraries. The following is the necessary code we need to include in our HTML file:

```
<script src="lib/jasmine-2.3.0/jasmine.js"></script>
<script src="lib/jasmine-2.3.0/jasmine-html.js"></script>
<script src="lib/jasmine-2.3.0/boot.js"></script>
```

To style the page, we can use the CSS provided by Jasmine:

```
<link rel="stylesheet" type="text/css" href="lib/jasmine-
2.3.0/jasmine.css">
```

Jasmine keeps our JavaScript code and tests in different folders, src—for our logical code, and spec—for all the tests.

You would need to check the paths of the files as per your setup. A simple skeleton will be like this:

```
<!DOCTYPE html>
<html>
<head>
  <meta charset="utf-8">
  <title>Jasmine v2.3.0</title>

  <link rel="shortcut icon" type="image/png" href="lib/jasmine-
  2.3.0/jasmine_favicon.png">
  <link rel="stylesheet" href="lib/jasmine-2.3.0/jasmine.css">

  <script src="lib/jasmine-2.3.0/jasmine.js"></script>
  <script src="lib/jasmine-2.3.0/jasmine-html.js"></script>
  <script src="lib/jasmine-2.3.0/boot.js"></script>

  <script src="js/jquery.1.11.3.min.js"></script>

  <!-- include source files here... -->
  <script src="src/start.js"></script>

  <!-- include spec files here... -->
  <script src="spec/startSpec.js"></script>

</head>

<body>
</body>
</html>
</head>
```

In the preceding code, we included two more files except those required by Jasmine. One is start.js in the src/ folder, which contains our logical code, functions, and many more. Another one is startSpec.js, which contains our testing code. For now, we created a simple function to add two values in start.js.

```
// function to add two values.
function add(a, b){
  return a + b;
}
```

And we created our specs in the startSpec.js file in the spec folder.

```
describe("Title of a Suite",", function() {
    // variables available for all specs
    var numberA= 3;
    var numberB = 2;

    // the function 'it' defines a spec
    it("Testing the add() function", function() {
      expect(add(numberA, numberB)).toEqual(5);
    });

});
```

We added an expectation in the spec chained with a matcher toEqual(). This matcher is going to compare the values. You are going to learn expectations and matchers further in this chapter. For now, let's create a file (for example, testAdd. html) and see the output after we run the file. Open the browser and run testAdd. html to run the tests:

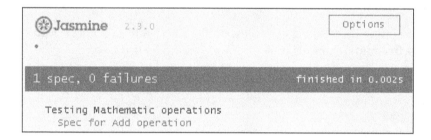

We can see the output that one spec was run and passed with zero failures.

Expectations

Assertions in Jasmine are named as an expectation. An expectation can either be true or false. Every expectation takes an actual value as only argument. An expectation is then chained with a matcher, which takes the expected value as an argument.

```
expect(true).toBe(true);
```

Here, expect is an expectation and toBe is a matcher. To evaluate negative assertions, expect() is chained with a not before calling a matcher. Matchers are used for Boolean comparison and validation of an expected value. You will learn more about matchers in the next subsection. See the following code:

```
expect(false).not.toBe(true);
```

Matchers

Matchers are used to compare the expected and actual values or validation of the expected value. If a matcher is going to compare the expected value, it takes actual value as argument. Matchers are chained with expectations. There are a number of matchers provided by Jasmine. Here is a list of all matchers:

- `toBe()`: This matcher compares using the identity (= = =) operator.

  ```
  var a = 5;
  expect(a).toBe(5);
  expect(a).not.toBe("5");
  ```

  The difference between the identity operator (= = =) and equality operator (= =) is that in identity operator, no type conversion is done before comparison.

- `toEqual()`: This matcher is used to compare simple literals, variables, and functions.

  ```
  expect(a).toEqual(5); // checking for simple variables.
  expect(a).not.toEqual(3);
  ```

  For simple literals and variables, both `toBe()` and `toEqual()` can be used, but to compare objects only `toEqual()` is to be used.

- `toMatch()`: This matcher is used for regular expressions.

  ```
  var strReg = "The quick brown fox";

  expect(strReg).toMatch(/The/);
  expect(strReg).not.toMatch(/jump/);
  ```

- `toBeDefined()`: This matcher checks if a variable or a function is defined. Let's check for the function we defined for addition:

  ```
  expect(add).toBeDefined(); // will pass
  expect(add).not.toBeDefined(); // will not pass
  ```

- `toBeUndefined()`: This matcher does the opposite of `toBeDefined()`.

  ```
  expect(add).toBeUndefined(); // will not pass
  expect(add).not.toBeUndefined(); // will pass
  ```

- `toBeNull()`: This matcher checks if a variable is `null`.

  ```
  expect(a).not.toBeNull();
  expect(null).toBeNull();
  ```

- `toBeTruthy()`: This matcher checks if a variable or expression is `true`.
  ```
  a = false;
  b = true;
  expect(b).toBeTruthy();
  expect(a).not.toBeTruthy();
  expect(add(2,3)).toBeTruthy();
  ```

- `toBeFalsy()`: This matcher checks if a value or expression is `false`.
  ```
  expect(add(0,0)).toBeFalsy();
  expect(b).not.toBeFalsy();
  ```

- `toContain()`: This matcher checks if a collection (array) has an item or not.
  ```
  var fruits = ["apple", "orange", "grape","papaya", "peach",
  "banana" ];
  expect(fruits).toContain("apple");
  ```

- `toBeLessThan()`: This matcher is for the comparison of numbers in mathematics.
  ```
  var a = 2, b = 3, c = 5.1234;
  expect(a).toBeLessThan(b);
  expect(c).not.toBeLessThan(a);
  ```

  In the first expect statement, it compares a to b and expects b would be greater than a. While in next statement, it expects c would not be less than a.

- `toBeGreaterThan()`: This matcher is the opposite of `toBeLessThan()`.
  ```
  expect(b).toBeGreaterThan(a);
  expect(b).not.toBeGreaterThan(c);
  ```

- `toBeCloseTo()`: This matcher checks if a number is close to another number. This matcher takes two arguments, the first is the number and second is the decimal precision. Let's see the following example to understand this matcher:
  ```
  expect(c).toBeCloseTo(5.1, 1) // will pass
  expect(c).not.toBeCloseTo(5.1, 2) // will pass
  ```

  Since c has a value 5.1234, it is compared to 5.1 that matches till the first digit. Thus, it passes for the first expectation.

- `toThrow()`: This matcher checks if a function throws an exception.
  ```
  f1 = function() {
      return 1 + 2;
  };
  f2 = function() {
  ```

```
    return undefinedVar + 1;
};

expect(f1).not.toThrow();
expect(f2).toThrow();
```

- `toThrowError()`: This matcher checks if an specific exception was thrown from a function.

```
f3 = function() {
    throw new TypeError("A custom Exception from f3");
};

expect(f3).toThrowError("custom");
```

The preceding expectation will fail, as the strings do not match exactly. `"custom"` does not match `"A custom Exception from f3"`. But the following expectation will pass, because it uses regular expression to match the strings:

```
expect(f3).toThrowError(/custom/);
```

The following expectation checks using the exception type as well. It also takes an optional argument as a string or regular expression to match the string.

```
expect(f3).toThrowError(TypeError); // will pass, checks
type
expect(f3).toThrowError(TypeError, /custom/); // will pass
expect(f3).toThrowError(TypeError, "custom exception"); //
will fail
```

- `jasmine.any()`: Sometimes, we are unaware of the actual value of an expression, but know the type. In this case, we can match them using `jasmine.any()`. Let's see how this is used:

```
expect([12,323]).toEqual(jasmine.any(Array));
expect({}).toEqual(jasmine.any(Object));
expect(21312312).toEqual(jasmine.any(Number));
```

As we can see, `jasmine.any` will match the expected value to a type of class.

- `jasmine.objectContaining()`: We can also do partial match when it comes to key/pair values. Let's see the following example to see how it works:

```
var employee = {
    name: "Alice",
    age: 29,
    department: "Testing",
```

```
      grade: 5
    }
    expect(employee).toEqual(jasmine.objectContaining({
      department: "Testing"
    }));
    expect(employee).toEqual(jasmine.objectContaining({
      age: jasmine.any(Number)
    }));
```

We can provide a key/value pair to match partially with an object. Sometimes, these default matchers are not enough to fulfill our requirements, and we need to create custom matchers. With Jasmine, we can create custom matchers, which you will learn later in this chapter.

Set up and tear down

Just like other frameworks, Jasmine also provides a way to set up and tear down. Jasmine provides global functions such as beforeEach—called before each spec, afterEach—called after each spec, beforeAll—called only once before all specs are run, and afterAll—called only once after all specs are done. Look at the following code to understand this:

```
describe("Setup and Teardown", function() {
  var count = 0;
  var velocity = 0;
  beforeEach(function() {
    velocity = 100;
    count++;
    console.log("Count is "+ count);
  });

  afterEach(function() {
    velocity = 0;
    console.log("Some spec just finished and this function is
    called");
  });

  beforeAll(function(){
    console.log("This is called only once, specs are about to
    run.");
  });

  afterAll(function(){
    console.log("All specs finished, time for cleanup");
```

```
  });

  it("Testing Velocity and reducing velocity", function() {
    expect(velocity).toEqual(100);
    velocity = 20;
    expect(velocity).toBe(20);
  });

  it("Testing Velocity", function() {
    expect(velocity).toEqual(100);
    expect(true).toEqual(true);
  });

});
```

If you run the following code, you will see all specs running successfully with status pass and the following will be the console output:

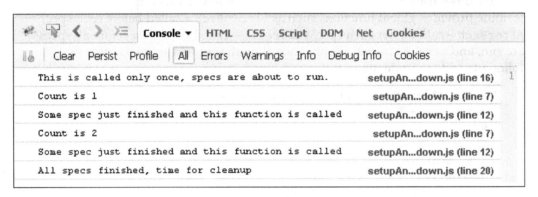

The `beforeAll` and `afterAll` functions are run once during a run. We can see that the variable `count` is increased by 1 before each spec is run and velocity is set to `100` so that the first expectation of each spec is met true.

This was one way of sharing variables among `it`, `beforeEach`, and `afterEach`. There is one more way using the `this` keyword, which is set to empty for each spec. Consider the following code:

```
describe("Setup and Teardown using this keyword", function() {
  beforeEach(function() {
    this.velocity = 100;
  });

  afterEach(function() {
    this.velocity = 0;
```

```
  });

  it("Testing Velocity", function() {
    expect(this.velocity).toEqual(100);
    this.velocity = 20;
    expect(this.velocity).toBe(20);
    this.acceleration = 5;
  });

  it("Testing acceleration", function(){
    expect(this.acceleration).toBeUndefined();
  });
});
```

Since the `this` keyword will be set to empty for the next spec, `this.acceleration` will not be defined. Running this suite will pass all the specs in it.

Spies

A **spy** is an emulation of a function or object, irrespective of which function/object is defined or not. There are times when we need stubs for the functions we need to use for performing testing. Jasmine has spies for this purpose. A spy can stub functions but can only exist within `describe` and `it` block if it is defined.

Apart from the matchers we read in this chapter, there are special matchers just for spies. One is `toHaveBeenCalled()`, which returns `true` if the spy was called. Another one is `toHaveBeenCalledWith()`, which returns `true` if the spy was called with arguments.

Let's see the following example to understand how spies work. The following is our source for an `Employee` function in the `employee.js` file created in the `src` folder:

```
var DEFAULT_SALARY = 1000;

function Employee(name, grade, department, salary) {
    this.name = name;
    this.grade   = grade;
    this.department = department;

    this.salary = salary || 0;
}
```

```
Employee.prototype.getName = function() {
    return this.name;
};

Employee.prototype.getDepartment = function() {
    return this.department;
};

Employee.prototype.getGrade = function() {
    return this.grade;
};

Employee.prototype.getSalary = function() {
    return this.salary;
};

Employee.prototype.calculateSalary = function() {
    return this.grade * DEFAULT_SALARY;
};

Employee.prototype.getDetails = function() {
    return 'Employee Name: ' + this.getName() + "\nDepartment: " +
    this.getDepartment() + '\nGrade: ' + this.getGrade() +
        '\nSalary: ' + this.getSalary();
};
```

We need to print details of each employee. We want to be sure that the salary was calculated before employee details were printed. We create a spy using the spyOn() function and call this file spyEmployee.js. We then put it in the spec folder.

```
describe("Jasmine Spy", function() {

  it("Spying employee", function(){
    var alice = new Employee("Alice", 4, "Testing");
    spyOn(alice, "calculateSalary");
    console.log(alice.getDetails());
    expect(alice.calculateSalary).toHaveBeenCalled();
  });

});
```

We created a spy using `spyOn(alice, "calculateSalary")`, and then called the `toHaveBeenCalled()` matcher. As soon as we create a spy on the `calculateSalary()` function, Jasmine replaces the actual implementation. Now a spy will be called rather than an actual implementation.

Put it all together in an HTML file called `spyEmployee.html`.

```html
<!DOCTYPE html>
<html>
<head>
  <meta charset="utf-8">
  <title>Jasmine v2.3.0</title>

  <link rel="shortcut icon" type="image/png" href="lib/jasmine-
  2.3.0/jasmine_favicon.png">
  <link rel="stylesheet" href="lib/jasmine-2.3.0/jasmine.css">

  <script src="lib/jasmine-2.3.0/jasmine.js"></script>
  <script src="lib/jasmine-2.3.0/jasmine-html.js"></script>
  <script src="lib/jasmine-2.3.0/boot.js"></script>

  <script src="js/jquery.1.11.3.min.js"></script>

  <!-- include source files here... -->
  <script src="src/employee.js"></script>

  <!-- include spec files here... -->
  <script src="spec/spyEmployee.js"></script>

</head>

<body>
</body>
</html>
```

After running this HTML file, the following is the output:

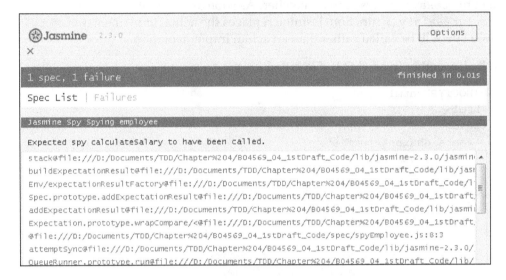

As we can see, it was expected that `calculateSalary` should have been called, but it failed since it was not called before printing the salary. Now let's change our code in `employee.js` and keep spec as it is:

```
var DEFAULT_SALARY = 1000;

function Employee(name, grade, department, salary) {
    this.name = name;
    this.grade  = grade;
    this.department = department;

    this.salary = salary || 0;
}
Employee.prototype.getName = function() {
    return this.name;
};

Employee.prototype.getDepartment = function() {
    return this.department;
};

Employee.prototype.getGrade = function() {
    return this.grade;
};
```

```
Employee.prototype.getSalary = function() {
    if(!this.salary){
        this.salary = this.calculateSalary();
    }
    return this.salary;
};

Employee.prototype.calculateSalary = function() {
    return this.grade * DEFAULT_SALARY;
};

Employee.prototype.printDetails = function() {
    return 'Employee Name: ' + this.getName() + "\nDepartment: " +
    this.getDepartment() + '\nGrade: ' + this.getGrade() +
        '\nSalary: ' + this.getSalary();
};
```

As we can see, `calculateSalary` is now being called from the `getSalary()` function. Let's run this again and see what happens:

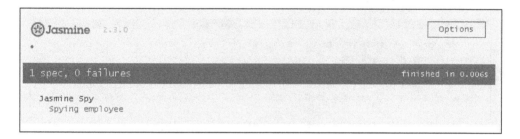

Now spec passed because it could find that the salary was calculated before printing details. In this example, we worked with the `toHaveBeenCalled()` matcher. There are several other matchers also defined for spies:

- `toHaveBeenCalledWith()`: To understand this, let's modify method in `employee.js`:

    ```
    Employee.prototype.calculateSalary = function(grade){
        this.grade = grade;
        this.salary = this.grade * DEFAULT_SALARY;
    }
    ```

This method will take grade and set both the salary and grade for an employee. We know that it will call the `calculateSalary()` function without any argument, which we can see by our implementation. We add one more spec to check if this was called with or without arguments.

```
it("Spying employee with arguments", function(){
    var alice = new Employee("Alice", 4, "Testing");
    spyOn(alice, "calculateSalary");
    alice.printDetails();
    expect(alice.calculateSalary).toHaveBeenCalledWith(5);
});
```

If we run our spec now, we can see that it will fail with message: **Expected spy calculateSalary to have been called with [5] but actual calls were [ ]**:

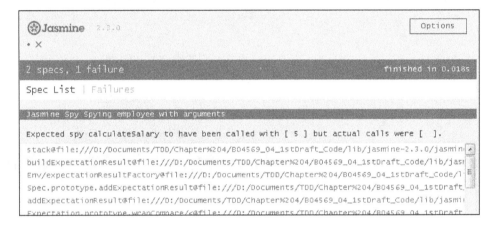

We can chain the expectation with `not` as well:

```
expect(alice.calculateSalary).not.toHaveBeenCalledWith(5);
```

After chaining with `not`, if you rerun the spec, it will pass.

- `callThrough()`: Jasmine replaces actual implementation of a function on which `spyOn()` is called. Sometimes, there is a need of getting the actual output of a function. Chaining `spyOn()` with `and.callThrough()`, it is possible to run the actual implementation of a function. Using `and.through()` with `spyOn()`, makes our spec implementation as follows:

```
it("Spying employee with call through", function(){
    var alice = new Employee("Alice", 4, "Testing");
    spyOn(alice, "calculateSalary").and.callThrough();
    var salary = alice.getSalary();
```

```
expect(alice.calculateSalary).toHaveBeenCalled();
console.log("Salary is :" + salary);
expect(salary).toEqual(4000);
});
```

The spec will pass since the `calculateSalary()` function was actually called inside `getSalary()`.

- `returnValue()`: There are times when we want to always return a specific value from a function. In this case, after creating spy, we can chain it with `and.returnValue()`, which takes a value as an argument that will be returned. The following is the example of using `returnValue()`:

```
it("Spying employee with return value", function(){
    var alice = new Employee("Alice", 4, "Testing");
    spyOn(alice, "calculateSalary").and.returnValue(9999);
    alice.calculateSalary();
    expect(alice.calculateSalary).toHaveBeenCalled();
    expect(alice.calculateSalary()).toEqual(9999);
});
```

This spec will pass since the return value of `calculateSalary()` will always be `9999` in any case. This is helpful in cases when there are calls made to remote services via AJAX or any other means. Returning data takes time, and you want to make it skip the service calls.

- `callFake()`: Sometimes, we may want to provide our own implementation of a function because the actual implementation takes time to execute or can be some other reason. In such cases, we can chain `spyOn()` with `and.callFake()`. `callFake()` takes a function as an argument, which is our implementation for the actual function name. The following spec will pass with this implementation:

```
it("Spying employee with a fake call", function(){
    var alice = new Employee("Alice", 4, "Testing");
    spyOn(alice,
    "calculateSalary").and.callFake(function(grade){
        var tSalary = 1000;
        return tSalary*grade;
    });
    var salary = alice.calculateSalary(10);
    expect(alice.calculateSalary).toHaveBeenCalled();
    expect(salary).toEqual(10000);
});
```

- `throwError()`: When we want a function to throw an error, we can chain `spyOn` with `and.throwError()`, which takes a string as an argument that will be thrown upon call. In the following spec, we can see that `calculateSalary` is spied with the throw error and error `"Service is down"` is thrown when it is being called:

```
it("Spying employee with throw error", function(){
    var alice = new Employee("Alice", 4, "Testing");
    spyOn(alice, "calculateSalary").and.throwError("Service
    is down");

    expect(alice.calculateSalary).toThrowError("Service is
    down");
});
```

- `stub()`: There may be times when `callThrough()` is used already, but we want only stub to be called and not the actual implementation. In this case, we can use `and.stub()` as in the following code:

```
it("Spying employee with call through and stub",
function(){
    var alice = new Employee("Alice", 4, "Testing");

    spyOn(alice, "calculateSalary").and.callThrough();
    var salary = alice.getSalary();
    console.log("Salary is: "+salary);

    console.log("Now calling stub");
    alice.calculateSalary.and.stub();
});
```

After the call to `stub()`, the effect of `callThrough()` will be removed.

Tracking spies using calls

There are several ways a spy can be tracked. For example, we can track if a spy was called or not, how many times, it was called, its arguments, its most recent call or first call and many more. Each and every call to a spy is tracked using the `calls` property.

- `calls.any()`: This function returns `true` if a spy was called at least once, else returns `false` when a spy wasn't called at all.

- `calls.count()`: This function returns a count of how many times a spy was called.

- `calls.argsFor()`: This takes an index as an argument, which is call number. An array is returned with all the arguments passed to that call.

- `calls.allArgs()`: This function returns the arguments passed to all of the calls.

- `calls.all()`: This one returns the context and arguments passed to all of the calls.

- `calls.mostRecent()`: This function returns the context and arguments passed to the most recent call.

- `calls.first()`: This one returns the context and arguments passed to first call made to the spy.

- `calls.reset()`: This function resets/clears all tracking properties for a spy.

Let's see all of these in action:

```
it("Tracking spies with calls property",function(){
  var alice = new Employee("Alice", 4, "Testing");

    spyOn(alice, "calculateSalary").and.callThrough();
    var salary = alice.getSalary();   // calls calculateSalary

    alice.calculateSalary.and.stub();
    salary = alice.getSalary();   // calls calculateSalary only if
    salary is zero
    expect(salary).toEqual(4000);

    expect(alice.calculateSalary.calls.any()).toEqual(true);
    expect(alice.calculateSalary.calls.count()).toEqual(1);
    console.log(alice.calculateSalary.calls.argsFor(0)); //
    returns blank []
    expect(alice.calculateSalary.calls.argsFor(0)).toEqual([]);

    alice.calculateSalary(1000);

    console.log(alice.calculateSalary.calls.argsFor(1)); //
    returns array [1000]
    expect(alice.calculateSalary.calls.argsFor(1))
    .toEqual([1000]);
    console.log(alice.calculateSalary.calls.allArgs()); // returns
    [[], [1000]]
    expect(alice.calculateSalary.calls.allArgs()).toEqual([[],
    [1000]]);
```

```
console.log(alice.calculateSalary.calls.all()); // returns
objects
console.log(alice.calculateSalary.calls.mostRecent());
console.log(alice.calculateSalary.calls.first());

alice.calculateSalary.calls.reset();

expect(alice.calculateSalary.calls.any()).toEqual(false);


});
```

All of these expectations are true and spec passes without fail. Output in the console would be as follows:

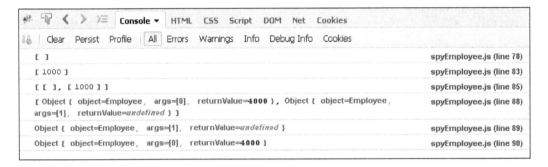

Creating a custom spy

We can create our own spy using the `createSpy()` function. This might be useful when we want to completely replace the original implementation and keep a stub or when there is no function defined yet to be spied upon. This spy will act as any other spy, and everything applies to it, for example, it can have arguments, it can be tracked, and so on. Let's see the following example:

```
describe("Custom spy", function(){

  var alice;

  beforeEach(function(){
    alice = new Employee("Alice", 5, "Testing");

    // creating a new spy for yet undefined function assignTask()
    alice.assignTask = jasmine.createSpy("assignTask");
```

```
    alice.getName =
    jasmine.createSpy("getName").and.returnValue("Ms Alice");

});

it("Expect assignTask to be defined",function(){
  expect(alice.assignTask).toBeDefined();
});
it("Expect assignTask to be called",function(){
  alice.assignTask();
  expect(alice.assignTask.calls.any()).toEqual(true);
});

it("Expect assignTask to be called with arguments",function(){
  alice.assignTask("Test the login of application");
  expect(alice.assignTask.calls.argsFor(0)).toEqual(["Test the
  login of application"]);
});

it("Expect name to be with title Mr or Ms", function(){
  console.log(alice.getName());
  expect(alice.getName()).toEqual("Ms Alice");
})
});
```

In the example, we created spy for a function named `assignTask` and tested it with various expectations. We also created a spy for `getName` to replace its original implementation. We can see after running the example that all of our expectations pass. We put this in a new spec file `customSpy.js` and include in our HTML file and run it.

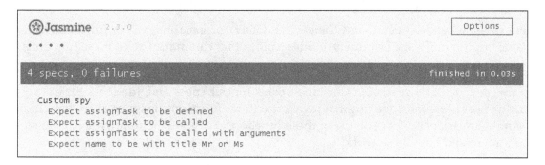

As we can see, all our specs passed. This is the way we can use `jasmine.createSpy` to create a custom spy. There is one more method, which will create an object with several methods. Using `createSpyObj()`, we can create a mock with multiple spies. Let's see the following spec to understand how it is created:

```
describe("Custom spy object", function(){
  var car;
  beforeEach(function(){
    car = jasmine.createSpyObj('car',
    ['start','stop','openDoor']);
    car.start();
    car.stop();
    car.openDoor();
  });

  it("Expect car to be started",function(){
    expect(car.start).toHaveBeenCalled();
  });
  it("Expect car to be stopped",function(){
    expect(car.start).toHaveBeenCalled();
  });

});
```

As we can see, `createSpyObj()` takes two arguments, first is the type or class and second is an array of strings. All of the strings in the array act as functions for which spies are created. In the previous example, a type car was created with three spies. All of these spies act as any other spy.

Jasmine clock

For cases, when we need to use the `setTimeout()` or `setInterval()` functions of JavaScript in our tests: Jasmine provides a clock that can make use of these functions available.

`jasmine.clock().install()` installs a clock for our specs and `jasmine.clock().uninstall()` restores the original JavaScript timer functions. Jasmine clock helps us handle time-dependent code using these functions. Let's see the following examples to understand how these work.

Suppose we want to check if Alice, an employee, was available after an hour, we create a spy for the `checkAvailabity()` function for an `employee` object:

```
var employee;

beforeEach(function() {
  employee = new Employee("Alice", 5, "Testing");
  employee.checkAvailability = jasmine.
  createSpy("checkAvailability");
  jasmine.clock().install();
});

afterEach(function() {
  jasmine.clock().uninstall();
});
```

We installed clock in `beforeEach()` and uninstalled it in `afterEach()` so that the original JavaScript timer functions are restored. In the next spec, we are going to use `setTimeout()`, which will be called once.

```
it("Checks if Alice is available after one hour", function() {

  // setting timeout for an hour
  setTimeout(function() {
    employee.checkAvailability()
  }, 60 * 60 * 1000);

  expect(employee.checkAvailability).not.toHaveBeenCalled();

  // need to tick clock for 1 hour = 60 * 60 * 1000 milliseconds
  jasmine.clock().tick(60 * 60 * 1000);

  expect(employee.checkAvailability).toHaveBeenCalled();
});
```

The original behavior of `setTimeout()` will call `employee.checkAvailability()` after one hour. Jasmine spec is not going to wait till then, but it will assume that it was called after an hour. We use the `jasmine.clock.tick()` function to move the clock forward. This function takes milliseconds as an argument and will tick the clock to the specified milliseconds. All these calls go synchronously. To understand this further, let's see next spec, which uses `setInterval()`:

```
it("Checks if Alice is available for next 3 hours", function() {
  setInterval(function() {
    employee.checkAvailability();
  }, 60 * 60 * 1000);
```

```
    expect(employee.checkAvailability).not.toHaveBeenCalled();

    jasmine.clock().tick(60 * 60 * 1000 + 1);
    expect(employee.checkAvailability.calls.count()).toEqual(1);

    jasmine.clock().tick(60 * 60 * 1000 + 1);
    expect(employee.checkAvailability.calls.count()).toEqual(2);

    jasmine.clock().tick(60 * 60 * 1000 + 1);
    expect(employee.checkAvailability.calls.count()).toEqual(3);
});
```

In this spec, `employee.checkAvailability()` will be called after each hour. After each call, we ticked clock to an hour + 1 millisecond, and function is called again. These are useful when we need synchronous calls and want some specific object or value to be modified after each function call or in case of some service calls.

Creating a custom matcher

In *Chapter 2, Testing Concepts*, we read that unit tests act as documentation to the project. In order for them to be descriptive, success and failure messages of tests should be very clear. But, sometimes, the default matchers as explained previously, are not sufficient or leave us with unexpected, unclear messages when fail or pass. For example, our expectation is:

```
expect(employee.salary).toEqual(9000);
```

This results in failure because the actual salary was 4,000.

```
Expected 1000 to equal 9000.
```

By looking at the message, you cannot detect what the context was. How about if it was something like: `"Expected salary of employee was 9000 but found to be 4000"`. This message gives us an idea from the message itself that the salary calculated must be wrong. To overcome this, Jasmine supports a creation of custom matchers.

Suppose we have a large number of employees in the context of a project and we need to check if an employee has marked his/her attendance daily. Our development requirements need to check if the employee is present on a particular day or not, and this is checked in the code from a good number of times.

In this case, there is a property for each `employee` object, which holds the status-code of attendance on a daily basis. The following table shows the status code versus status:

Code	Status
0	Not present
1	Present
2	On leave
3	Half day(first half present)
4	Half day(second half present)
5	Left organization permanently

To check if the employee is present full time, the following expectation would be good if it is rarely used in the project:

```
expect(employee.get('attendanceStatus')).toEqual(1);
```

But what if it was like this:

```
expect(employee).toBePresentToday();
```

Sounds good, doesn't it? This is descriptive, clear, and serves the purpose. Let's create a custom matcher for this.

First, let's modify our `employee.js` for attendance so that we can use it for our matcher:

```
Employee.prototype.markAttendance = function(status){
   this.attendanceStatus = status;
};
Employee.prototype.getAttendance = function(){
   return this.attendanceStatus;
};
```

A custom matcher can also take an actual value and an optional expected value. Here, we are going to keep only one as we need only employee for which we will check internally for the status. Our custom matcher is:

```
var customMatchers = {
   toBePresent: function(util, customEqualityTesters){
      return{
compare : function(employee){
```

```
var statusCode = employee.getAttendance();
var result = {};
result.pass = util.equals(statusCode, 1 ,
customEqualityTesters);
if(result.pass){
  result.message = "Employee "+employee.getName()+" is
  present today";
}else{
  result.message = "Employee "+employee.getName()+" is
  absent today";
}
return result;
  }

  }
 }
}
```

We created a `customMatchers` array, which will hold all of our custom matchers. Then, we create a matcher `isEmployeePresent()`. While creating it, we give it two arguments, `util` and `customEqualityTesters`, that have a set of utility functions, which a matcher can use. Any call to `util.equal()` inside matcher needs a `customEqualityTesters` variable, which is second argument to the function. Then, we return the result of a `compare` function. This `compare` function does the actual comparison between values using the `util.equals()` function call.

To use this matcher, in the `beforeEach()` block of our suite in `describe`, we register this matcher using `jasmine.addMatchers(customMatchers)`. Once registered, it will be available for any expectation in the block.

Our suite goes as follows:

```
describe("Custom Matcher", function(){

  beforeEach(function(){
    jasmine.addMatchers(customMatchers);
  });

  it("Expected employee to be present ", function(){
    var alice = new Employee("Alice", 5, "Testing");
    alice.markAttendance(2);
    console.log(alice);
    expect(alice).toBePresent();
  });
});
```

All our custom matchers and suites go in the same file named `customMatchers.js`. Upon execution, our spec will fail, but the message will be descriptive and clear:

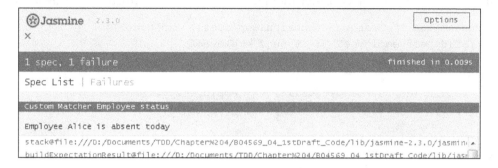

As we can see, the custom message now appears after the execution. For negative equality check, we can chain expectations with a not just like default matchers. In that case, our expectation would be:

```
expect(alice).not.toBePresent();
```

This is how a custom matcher is created and used. They behave like any other matcher. We passed only one argument to compare the function in matcher. In case we want to compare a user given actual and expected value, we just need to modify the function signature to two arguments and use the other argument for comparison.

Creating a custom equality tester

Sometimes, you may want to compare two values or objects in your way. By defining a custom equality tester, you can modify how Jasmine determines if two values are equal or not.

Whenever an expectation needs to check for equality, custom equality tester will first be used. It would return true or false if it knows how to compare; otherwise, undefined will be returned. If undefined is returned, then only Jasmine's default equality testers will be used.

Let's modify `employee.js` once more to add setter getter for the e-mail so that we can use in our custom equality tester:

```
Employee.prototype.setEmail = function(email){
  this.email = email;
}
Employee.prototype.getEmail = function(){
  return this.email;
}
```

To create a custom equality tester, we create a function which takes two arguments. Let's create an equality tester for employees. If two employee objects have same e-mail and name, we will consider them to be equal. So, our function goes as follows:

```
customEqualityTester = function(employee1, employee2){
  if(typeof employee1 !== typeof employee2 ){
    return false;
  }
  return (employee1.getEmail() === employee2.getEmail()) &&
(employee1.getName() === employee2.getName())
};
```

Now when we have our function ready, we can register this function in `beforeEach()` using `jasmine.addCustomEqualityTester()`. After registration, this will be available, and we can use this in our specs. Let's put it all together in the `customEquality.js` file and run:

```
customEqualityTester = function(employee1, employee2){
  if(typeof employee1 !== typeof employee2 ){
    return false;
  }
  return (employee1.getEmail() === employee2.getEmail()) &&
(employee1.getName() === employee2.getName())
}

describe("Checking Employee equality tester", function(){
  var employeeA, employeeB;
  beforeEach(function(){
    jasmine.addCustomEqualityTester(customEqualityTester);

    employeeA = new Employee("Alice", 5, "Testing");
    employeeA.setEmail("alice@example.com");
    employeeB = new Employee("Alice", 4, "Development");
    employeeB.setEmail("alice@example.com");
  });

  it("Should be equal", function(){
    expect(employeeA).toEqual(employeeB);
  });
  it("Should not be equal", function(){
    var employeeC = new Employee("Bob", 5, "Testing");
    employeeC.setEmail("bob@example.com");
    expect(employeeA).not.toEqual(employeeC);
  });
});
```

The output of the execution would be:

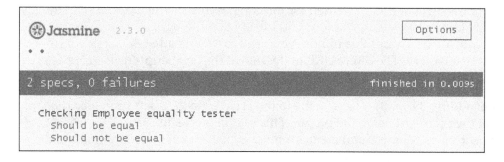

This is how we can extend Jasmine to use our own equality testers.

Asynchronous calls

There are websites, which heavily use AJAX calls to collect and present data. In such cases, it's useful to mock AJAX calls to make testing easy. But sometimes, actual AJAX calls are required, and with Jasmine, we can use asynchronous calls in our specs. Calls to `beforeEach()`, `afterEach()`, and `it()` can take an optional argument, `done`. This `done()` function should be called when asynchronous operations are completed:

```
beforeEach(function(done) {
  // some asynchronous operation
  done();();
});
```

Once our operations are done, we call the `done()` function in `beforeEach()`:

```
it("should perform some asynchronous operations", function(done) {
  // asynchronous operations
  // expectations
  done();
});
```

This spec will not be called until the `done()` function in `beforeEach()` is called and this spec will not complete until `done` is called in spec. By default Jasmine will wait for 5 seconds to complete asynchronous operation, in case we need more time or want to set less time, we can do this using `jasmine.DEFAULT_TIMEOUT_INTERVAL`. We can set this to the time as per our requirement. One important thing to note is that this this interval should be reset to Jasmine's default interval after spec is completed. So, if suppose it was set to 10 seconds in `beforeEach()`, we should set it to 5 seconds in `afterEach()`.

The Jasmine Ajax plugin

Jasmine also has a plugin written for mocking asynchronous operations. The plugin jasmine-ajax is available at GitHub at `https://github.com/pivotal/jasmine-ajax`. To add this plugin, you need to download `mock-ajax.js` from the `lib` directory. The direct URL to download the JavaScript file is `https://raw.githubusercontent.com/jasmine/jasmine-ajax/master/lib/mock-ajax.js`.

After adding the `mock-ajax.js` file to the HTML file (let's say `testJasmineAjax.html`), we can start using the plugin. This plugin mocks the actual asynchronous behavior and creates a mock of `XMLHttpRequest` by creating the `FakeXMLHttpRequest` object.

If we want to provide AJAX support for the whole suite, we can add the `jasmine.Ajax.install()` function call to `beforeEach` the and `jasmine.Ajax.uninstall()` function call to `afterEach`.

```
describe("Using mock-ajax for Asynchronous operations testing",
function() {

  beforeEach(function() {
    jasmine.Ajax.install();
  });

  afterEach(function() {
    jasmine.Ajax.uninstall();
    });
});
```

A call to `jasmine.Ajax.uninstall()` is important; because of this call, Jasmine restores the original behavior of Ajax calls so that other specs or parts of code, which want to make real Ajax calls can continue.

Let's checkout the example spec, which uses async operation:

```
it("Checking weather report AJAX API", function() {
  var successFunction = jasmine.createSpy("success");
  var xhr = new XMLHttpRequest();
  xhr.onreadystatechange = function(args) {
    if (this.readyState == this.DONE) {
      successFunction(this.responseText);
    }
  };
```

```
xhr.open("GET", "/get/weather/IN-Mumbai");
xhr.send();

expect(jasmine.Ajax.requests.mostRecent().url)
.toBe('/get/weather/IN-Mumbai');
expect(successFunction).not.toHaveBeenCalled();
jasmine.Ajax.requests.mostRecent().respondWith({
    "status": 200,
    "contentType": 'text/plain',
    "responseText": 'Temp 25 C, Sunlight'
});
expect(successFunction).toHaveBeenCalledWith('Temp 25 C,
Sunlight');
});
```

In the preceding spec, we first create a spy for the `success` function, which can be used to call the `readyState` once. The `readyState` of Ajax request is equal to `DONE`. `jasmine.Ajax.requests.mostRecent()` returns the object of `FakeXMLHttpRequest`. After that, we can use a normal Ajax call as we generally do. `jasmine.Ajax.requests.MostRecent().url` holds the recently called URL. Since this is mocking, we also need to provide a response. In the response, we need to provide the status, `contentType` and `responseText`, which should be string.

These were the ways using which Jasmine allows to use actual AJAX calls or to mock AJAX calls in the specs.

Nesting suites

As a project matures, the unit testing code grows huge and it's difficult to maintain. In such cases, it's good to use nested suites. Consider an example of a company, where employees are classified into several departments such as admin, finance, HR, delivery, presales, and sales. While there can be a common set of specs that apply to all employees, each department may also need some specs for department-specific features. Desk allocation can be task related to admin, while annual prize distribution can be a part of HR. Now all these specs can be grouped into suites, and all these suites can be clubbed into one suite for the whole company. We can nest suites by placing a describe block into another describe:

```
describe("Testing Company wide functions", function(){
    describe("Testing HR department functions", function(){

        describe("Testing HR department functions - Prize
        Distribution", function(){
        });
```

```
describe("Testing HR department functions - Offer Letter
Distribution", function(){
});
describe("Testing HR department functions - New recruitment",
function(){
});
});
describe("Testing Admin department functions", function(){

  describe("Testing Admin department functions - Reception",
  function(){
  });
  describe("Testing Admin department functions - Pantry",
  function(){
  });
});
describe("Testing Finance department functions", function(){

  describe("Testing Finance department functions -
  Reimbursement", function(){
  });
  describe("Testing Finance department functions - Salary",
  function(){
  });
});

});
```

This allows suites to be like a tree of functions. When a spec is executed, it walks down the tree while executing each beforeEach(). Similarly after execution, the afterEach() functions are called.

To understand this, let's see the following example:

```
describe("Nested Suites - top suite", function(){
  var count = 0;
  beforeEach(function(){
    console.log("Count in top suite: "+count);
    count++;
  });
  afterEach(function(){
    console.log("Calling top afterEach");
  });
  it("Increases count", function(){
    console.log(count);
    expect(true).toEqual(true);
```

```
    });
    describe("Nested Suites - Inner suite", function(){
      beforeEach(function(){
        console.log("Count in Inner suite: "+count);
        count++;
      });
      afterEach(function(){
        console.log("Calling inner afterEach");
      });
      it("Increases count", function(){
        console.log("Count : " +count);
        expect(true).toEqual(true);
      });
      describe("Nested Suites - inner most suite", function(){
        beforeEach(function(){
          console.log("Count in inner most suite: "+count);
          count++;
        });
        afterEach(function(){
          console.log("Calling inner most afterEach");
        });
        it("Increases count", function(){
          console.log("Count : " +count);
          expect(true).toEqual(true);
        });
      });
    });
  });
```

When the inner most spec is called, the first top-most `beforeEach()` will be called, then the inner and inner-most `beforeEach()` will be called. Similar behavior is applicable for `afterEach()`. The output in the console log comes as follows:

```
Count in top suite: 0
Count : 1
Calling top afterEach
Count in top suite: 1
Count in Inner suite: 2
Count : 3
Calling inner afterEach
Calling top afterEach
Count in top suite: 3
Count in Inner suite: 4
Count in inner most suite: 5
```

```
Count : 6
Calling inner most afterEach
Calling inner afterEach
Calling top afterEach
```

Disabling suites and specs

Sometimes, we may want to run only specific set of suites and skip all others. Suites that we want to skip can be disabled using xdescribe. For example:

```
xdescribe("Disabled suite", function(){
  it("A spec", function(){
    expect(true).toBeTruthy();
  });
});
```

Similarly we can skip specs as well using xit:

```
describe("A suite", function() {
  it("A spec", function(){
    expect(true).toBeTruthy();
  });
  xit("Another spec", function(){

  });
  xit("Disabled spec", function(){

  });
});
```

Disabling is useful when we have so many specs created in a project, and we want to test only a specific functionality. It we put these all together and run, output will be as follows:

Jasmine has a way, which enables us to run only one suite or spec. Just like we added x before describe and it, this plugin allows us to prefix f. So, if a spec is defined by fit rather than it, suites are fdescribe rather than describe. These specs declared with fit are known as focused specs:

```
describe("A suite", function() {
    fit("focused spec and will run", function(){
        expect(true).toBeTruthy();
    });
    it("Spec will not run", function(){
        expect(true).toBeTruthy();
    });
    fdescribe("Focused suite", function() {
        it("Spec will run", function(){
            expect(true).toBeTruthy();
        });
    });
});
```

In the preceding code, any spec declared with fit will run, and all the specs inside fdescribe will run. The rest of the specs will not run and will be marked as disabled.

Another way to run only one spec/suite and skip all others is using the Jasmine test runner. By default, all suites and specs will run when the HTML file is loaded in a browser. We can click on one suite/spec to run only that suite/spec and skip the others. If the running suite has more suites inside, then all those suites will also run.

All disabled suite and specs will not run and be marked as faded color in the spec runner. These specs are also called pending specs. Any spec without any expectations will also be marked as pending in results.

Summary

Jasmine is considered to be very popular among testing frameworks. It is called to be complete and does not need any other supporting frameworks. In this chapter, you learned about the Jasmine testing framework and its offerings. You also learned how to extend Jasmine using custom spies, matchers, and equality testers with the help of the employee object.

In the next chapter, you will learn about JsTestDriver, its setup, and how we can run our Jasmine specs with it. We will also see how to perform Ajax operations in tests later in this book.

5

JsTestDriver

There are a number of tools available for running your tests. JsTestDriver is one of the most powerful ones. It can easily integrate to your project setup and your development environment. So far, you learned about popular frameworks to write your tests. JsTestDriver enables you to run tests of majority of these frameworks. You, in this chapter, will see how to use JsTestDriver with Jasmine, YUI frameworks as well as learn to see how to integrate it with your IDE.

The following topics will be covered in this chapter:

- JsTestDriver
- Integrating JsTestDriver with IDE
- Code coverage

JsTestDriver

We will first start with the overview about JsTestDriver, and then we will see that how we can set up the JsTestDriver.

Overview

Usually, most of the frameworks have their own browser-based test runners. While they are good, and since they use a browser to test, testing performed is actually done in a real environment. But that's not enough because you always need to test your code in more than one browser and not just one. You run the tests in each browser as per your requirements. JsTestDriver is one of the most powerful test runners. It can run tests on all browsers automatically, thus saving you from performing tests for each browser separately. JsTestDriver is an open source and written in Java.

JsTestDriver uses adapters to support other unit testing JavaScript frameworks. JsTestDriver has adapters available for:

- **QUnit**: `https://github.com/exnor/QUnit-to-JsTestDriver-adapter`
- **Jasmine**: `https://github.com/ibolmo/jasmine-jstd-adapter`
- **YUI Tests**: `https://github.com/fkowal/yuitest_jstestdriver`
- **Karma**: `https://www.npmjs.com/package/karma-jstd-adapter`

You will learn how to use Jasmine with the help of the Jasmine-jstd adapter later in this chapter.

Getting started

First thing first, let's get JsTestDriver, which is a JAR file. You can get it from the JsTestDriver app page hosted on `code.google.com`: `https://code.google.com/p/js-test-driver/downloads/detail?name=JsTestDriver-1.3.5.jar`.

Download the JAR file and put it in a directory. We will need to use the JAR file for our project directory.

Writing tests

Like any other testing framework, JsTestDriver also provides ways to write tests. There are two ways to write test cases, using prototype and inline declaration.

The following code snippet shows the prototype way of writing tests:

```
SimpleTest = TestCase("Very simple Tests");

SimpleTest.prototype.testOne = function(){
};

SimpleTest.prototype.testTwo = function(){
};
```

The following code snippet shows the inline declaration way of writing tests:

```
TestCase("Very simple Tests", {
    testOne: function(){
    }
    testTwo: function(){
    }
});
```

You will learn more on how to run our tests later in this chapter.

Assertions

JsTestDriver is not only a test runner, but also a testing framework as well. It also has a number of assertions to be used. Every assertion, takes a message as the first argument, which is to be displayed when it fails.

The following is the list of assertions provided by JsTestDriver:

- `assertTrue(message, actual)`: This checks if the result is true or not.
- `assertFalse(message, actual)`: This checks whether the result isn't false.
- `assertEquals(message, expected, actual)`: This checks whether the expected and actual values cannot be compared to be equal.
- `assertNotEquals(message, expected, actual)`: This checks whether the expected and actual values can be compared to be equal.
- `assertSame(message, expected, actual)`: This checks whether the expected and actual values are not references to the same object.
- `assertNotSame(message, expected, actual)`: This checks whether the expected and actual are references to the same object.
- `assertNull(message, actual)`: This checks whether the given value is not exactly null.
- `assertNotNull(message, actual)`: This checks whether the given value is exactly null.
- `assertUndefined(message, actual)`: This checks whether the given value is not undefined.
- `assertNotUndefined(message, actual)`: This checks whether the given value is undefined.
- `assertNaN(message, actual)`: This checks whether the given value is not a NaN.
- `assertNotNaN(message, actual)`: This checks whether the given value is a NaN.
- `assertException(message, callback, error)`: This checks whether the code in the callback does not throw the given error.
- `assertNoException(message, callback)`: This checks whether the code in the callback throws an error.
- `assertArray(message, actual)`: Checks whether the given value is not an array.
- `assertTypeOf(message, expected, value)`: This checks whether the JavaScript type of the value isn't the expected string.

- `assertBoolean(message, actual)`: This checks whether the given value is not a Boolean. Convenience function to `assertTypeOf`.

- `assertFunction(message, actual)`: This checks whether the given value is not a function. Convenience function to `assertTypeOf`.

- `assertObject(message, actual)`: This checks whether the given value is not an object. Convenience function to `assertTypeOf`.

- `assertNumber(message, actual)`: This checks whether the given value is not a number. Convenience function to `assertTypeOf`.

- `assertString(message, actual)`: This checks whether the given value is not a string. Convenience function to `assertTypeOf`.

- `assertMatch(message, regexp, actual)`: This checks whether the given value does not match the given regular expression.

- `assertNoMatch(message, regexp, actual)`: This checks whether the given value matches the given regular expression.

- `assertTagName(message, tagName, element)`: This checks whether the given DOM element is not of the given `tagName`.

- `assertClassName(message, className, element)`: This checks whether the given DOM element does not have a given CSS classname.

- `assertElementId(message, id, element)`: This checks whether the given DOM element does not have a given ID.

- `assertInstanceOf(message, constructor, actual)`: This checks whether the given object is not an instance of a given constructor.

- `assertNotInstanceOf(message, constructor, actual)`: This checks whether the given object is an instance of a given constructor.

- `fail(message)`: This throws a JavaScript error with a given message string.

Capturing the browser

We know that we can run our tests for multiple browsers; JsTestDriver can capture the browser to run tests. Let's see how this works. Open a command prompt in the directory where you put the JsTestDriver JAR file, pick a free port number like `9880` and run this command:

```
java -jar JsTestDriver-1.3.5.jar --port 9880
```

This will start a server on port `9880` keeping runner mode `QUIET` as you can see in the command prompt after running the command. Open a browser of your choice for example, Firefox, Chrome, and IE. In the browser, open `http://localhost:9880`. It will ask you to capture the browser, as seen in the following screenshot:

Click on the first link **Capture This Browser**, which will allow JsTestDriver to capture this browser:

Now Firefox is captured (in this case). If you open the same link in a different browser, it will also show you the number of captured browsers. Let's open `http://localhost:9880` in Google Chrome:

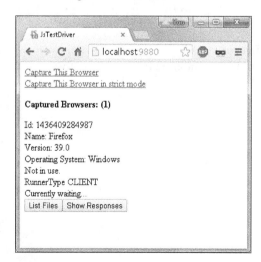

You can capture multiple browsers at the same time and JsTestDriver will use all the captured browsers to run the tests.

We can also capture the browsers giving their path in command line using the `--browser` flag.

```
java -jar JsTestDriver-1.3.5.jar --port 9880 --browser
firefoxpath,chromepath
```

Restructuring your project

Like most open source tools, JsTestDriver takes a configuration file to know, which JavaScript library to include, directory in which tests are present, along with several other configurations. You will learn about configuration later in this chapter.

Usually a web project contains a source directory and test directory. Inside the source directory, there will be `JavaScript`, `CSS`, `Images`, and so on, along with source files, which can be in any programming language such as PHP, Java. Our focus is going to be on JavaScript files and running the tests written for our JavaScript code.

There are four things that we define for any project in order to neatly configure it with JsTestDriver:

- **The source directory**: It is not strictly required, but recommended to create a source directory for an application. We will create the `src` directory here.

- **The test directory**: Again not strictly required, but it is a good practice to keep the test aside from the production code. We will name this directory as `src-test`.

- **The configuration file**: By default, the JsTestDriver runner will look for the `jsTestDriver.conf` file in the current directory. We need to keep same name for the configuration file.

- **The plugins directory**: We will keep all the plugins needed by JsTestDriver in this directory. We name it as the `lib` directory.

So, our directory structure will look as follows:

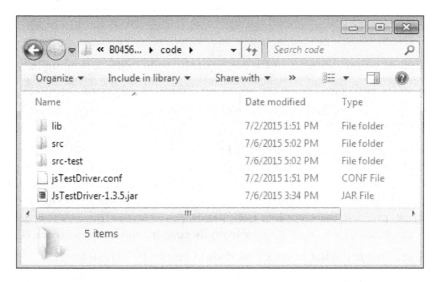

The configuration file

jsTestDriver.conf is a configuration file written in YAML syntax. There are number of options to use in this conf file:

```
server: http://localhost:9880

load:
  - src/*.js

test:
  - src-test/*.js

exclude:
 - not-to-be-used.js

serve:
 - css/main.css

proxy:
 - {matcher: "*", server: "http://localhost/my-proxy-server"}

plugin:
 - name: "coverage"
```

```
jar: "lib/coverage.jar"
module: "com.google.jstestdriver.coverage.CoverageModule"

timeout: 90
```

Let's see details about elements of the configuration file in the following list:

- `server`: This defines the default location of the server, it can be overridden using command line flags. We will see available the command line flags later in this chapter.

- `load`: This loads all the JavaScript files needed to run the tests. The `*.js` will load all the files in an alphabetical order. You can also provide a list of files to load, in that case, the files will be loaded as defined. This list should follow the YAML format to define the details. In case, you want to load an external script, provide the complete URL like `http://code.jquery.com/jquery-1.11.3.min.js` to load jQuery from its **content delivery network (CDN)**.

- `test`: This is the list of tests that should be run by JsTestDriver.

- `exclude`: In case we want to exclude some files from loading, we can mention them here.

- `serve`: This is used to load static content such as HTML, CSS, images, and so on.

- `proxy`: This enables JsTestDriver to behave as a proxy server. This can be useful when there are larger integration tests that need to communicate to a backend server.

- `plugin`: Here, we can mention the plugins to be used by JsTestDriver.

- `timeout`: This represents timeout in seconds.

Running tests using the command prompt

There are two ways to use the JsTestDriver runner. One is using command-line prompt and the other one is using an IDE. You will come to learn both approaches in this chapter. In this section, we will create a simple test and run it using the command line.

In the `src-test` directory, we create a test JavaScript file named `helloworld-test.js` and tests the function that we will create in our production code:

```
HelloWorldTest = TestCase("HelloWorldTest");
HelloWorldTest.prototype.testSay = function() {
    var helloWorldApp = new myapp.HelloWorldApp();
    assertEquals("Hello Reader!", helloWorldApp.say("Reader"));
};
```

In the `src` directory, let's create a JavaScript file named `helloworld.js` and a very simple function that takes an argument name and says hello to the name:

```
myapp = {};

myapp.HelloWorldApp = function() { };

myapp.HelloWorldApp.prototype.say = function(name) {
  return "Hello " + name + "!";
};
```

Recalling from the previous sections, we ran our server on port `9880`, and we are going to use the same server. We already captured the Firefox web browser for our testing purpose. Let's create a `jsTestDriver.conf` file in our project and mention the server URL, source, and tests files:

```
server: http://localhost:9880

load:
  - src/*.js

test:
  - src-test/*.js
```

We kept our `jsTestDriver.conf` file very simple and intended to load all the JavaScript files in the `src-test` and `src` directories.

Our server is in running mode, and we are capturing one browser so we can run test using the command-line prompt. Go to the directory where you have kept your project and open the command-line prompt. Run the command as shown to run the test:

```
java -jar JsTestDriver-1.3.5.jar --tests all
```

```
Administrator: C:\Windows\System32\cmd.exe

Microsoft Windows [Version 6.1.7601]
Copyright (c) 2009 Microsoft Corporation.  All rights reserved.

D:\B04569_05_1stDraft_Code\Command-Line>java -jar JsTestDriver-1.3.5.jar --tests all
setting runnermode QUIET
.
Total 1 tests (Passed: 1; Fails: 0; Errors: 0) (1.00 ms)
  Firefox 39.0 Windows: Run 1 tests (Passed: 1; Fails: 0; Errors 0) (1.00 ms)

D:\B04569_05_1stDraft_Code\Command-Line>_
```

In case we have multiple browsers captured, the console will show the output of all the browsers as shown in the following screenshot:

So far, we used only two flags in the command line `--tests` and `--port`. In fact, there are a number of flags, which we can use with the command line. To print all of the flags, try the following command:

```
java -jar JsTestDriver-1.3.5.jar --help
```

You should see a number of options mentioned here:

`--browser VAR`   : The path to the browser executable

`--browserTimeout VAR`   : The ms before a browser is declared dead.

`--captureAddress VAL`   : The address to capture the browser.

`--captureConsole`   : Capture the console (if possible) from the browser

`--config VAL`   : Loads the configuration file

`--dryRunFor VAR`   : Outputs the number of tests that are going to be run as well as their names for a set of expressions or all to see all the tests

`--help`   : Help

`--port N`   : The port on which to start the JsTestDriver server

`--preloadFiles`   : Preload the js files

`--raiseOnFailure VAL`   : Whether jstd will throw an exception when a test failure.

`--requiredBrowsers VAR`   : Browsers that all actions must be run on.

`--reset`   : Resets the runner

`--server VAL`   : The server to which to send the command

`--serverHandlerPrefix VAL` : Whether the handlers will be prefixed with jstd

```
--sslPort N                   : The SSL port on which to start the
JsTestDriver server

--testOutput VAL              : A directory to which serialize the results of
the tests as XML

--tests VAR                   : Run the tests specified in the form testCase.
testName

--verbose                     : Displays more information during a run

--plugins VAL[,VAL]           : Comma separated list of paths to plugin jars.

--config VAL                  : Path to configuration file.

--basePath VAL[,VAL]          : Override the base path(s) in the
configuration file. Defaults to the parent directory of the configuration
file.

--runnerMode VAL              : The configuration of the logging and
frequency that the runner reports actions: DEBUG, DEBUG_NO_TRACE, DEBUG_
OBSERVE, PROFILE, QUIET (default), INFO
```

Setting up JsTestDriver with IDE

In the previous section, we have seen how we can run JsTestDriver using command line. Now we will see how we can use it as an eclipse plugin. The eclipse plugin for JsTestDriver allows you to utilize all the features of JsTestDriver. Follow the steps to setup JsTestDriver for eclipse:

1. Install Eclipse Indigo version from `http://www.eclipse.org/downloads/download.php?file=/technology/epp/downloads/release/indigo/SR2/eclipse-jee-indigo-SR2-win32-x86_64.zip`.

2. Extract the downloaded ZIP in any of the drive of your system.

3. Start Eclipse and navigate to **Help** | **Install new Software**.

4. Add `http://js-test-driver.googlecode.com/svn/update/` as an update site as shown in the following screenshot:

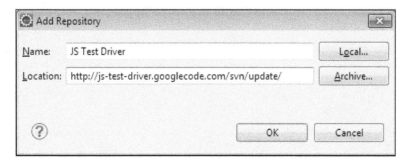

5. Check the **JS Test Driver Plugin for Eclipse** checkbox and hit **Next**:

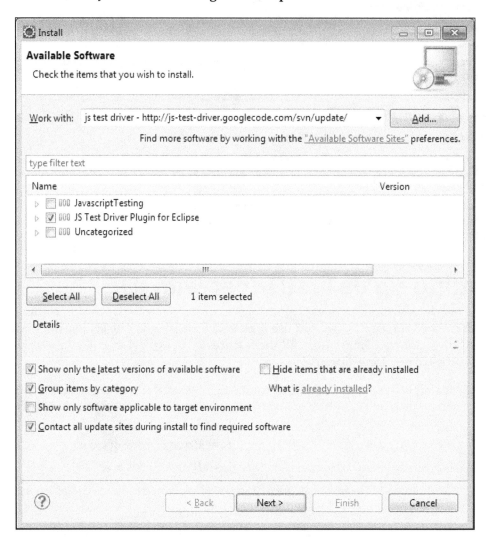

6. Click on **Next** on **Install Details** page:

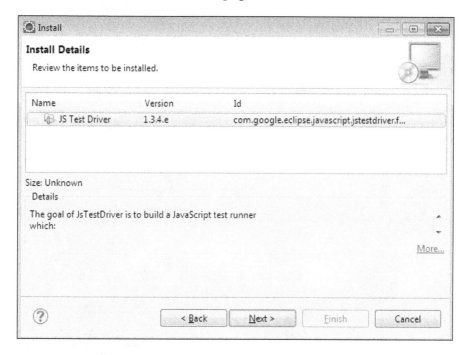

7. Accept the terms agreement and click on the **Finish** button.

8. You will get one security warning alert, then click on **Yes**.

9. When Eclipse asks you to restart/apply changes, click on **Restart**.

10. Now to allow Eclipse to install the JsTest driver for you, navigate to **Window | Show view | Other**, search for `jsTestDriver`, and select this view. You should see the view as in the following screenshot:

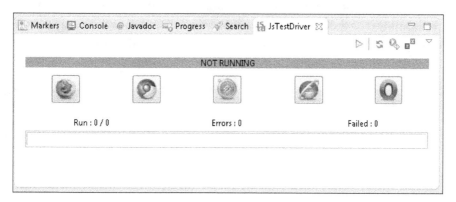

11. We also need to configure the plugin to make it useful. Navigate to Eclipse preferences and select **JS Test Driver** in left menu. We need to assign port and paths to browsers in the preferences. Let's choose the same port number 9880 and select the appropriate path for our browsers:

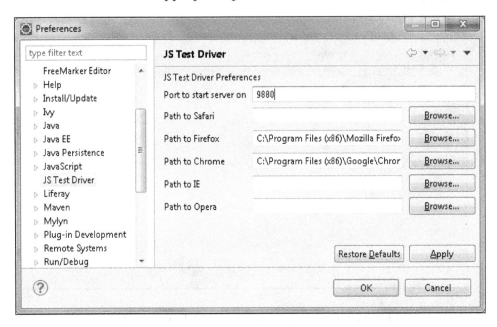

This plugin supports Safari, Firefox, Chrome, IE, and opera.

12. Let's run the server from the JsTestDriver panel shown in step 10. Click on the green play icon and the server should start. The browsers, for which we have set the paths, can open capture in the way we did previously or we can click on the icon to launch the browsers. Once a browser is captured, the browser icon will be active; otherwise, it will be gray. Also, if the server is running, the green bar will mention the URL to be used to capture the browser; else, it will show **NOT RUNNING** as in step 10.

If you see this, your eclipse has JsTestDriver installed and setup properly. They are ready to run tests in eclipse.

Running the tests

We will keep the same source and test files as used earlier in this chapter. We are going to test our HelloWorldApp. Let's create a simple eclipse JavaScript project using the same source:

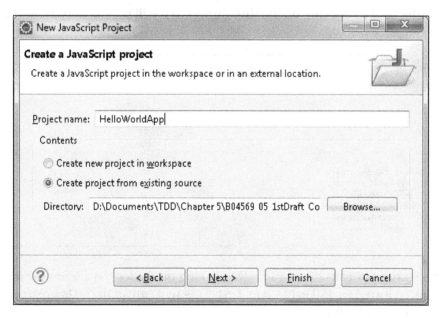

Once our project is set up, we can see all our code in the project explorer.

Let's navigate to **Run Configurations**, and then add a new JsTestDriver configuration. Simply select your project and configuration file as shown in the following screenshot:

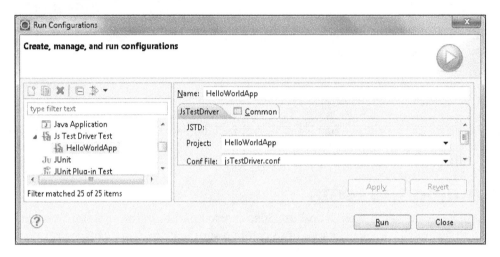

Let's run the tests by clicking on the **Run** button. We will see the output for the browsers as per the setup:

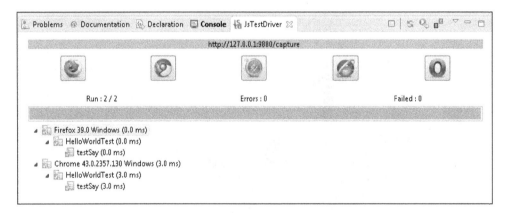

We can also run our tests by simply right-clicking on the test JavaScript file and navigating to **Run As | Js Test Driver Test**. This will run all the tests present in that file and show the report.

Similar to this, JsTestDriver can be integrated with other IDEs such as NetBeans and IntelliJIdea.

Running Jasmine specs

Normally in a project development, we pick a testing framework, write tests and production code, keep testing our test cases, and use some tool such as JsTestDriver. In this section, we will see how to setup and configure JsTestDriver with Jasmine and run our specs.

To add Jasmine support for our project, let's add Jasmine to the `src` folder. Download the `jasmine-1.1.0.js` file from `https://github.com/kravigupta/jasmine-1.1.0` at GitHub. After downloading, put the JS file in the `lib` directory of `HelloWorldApp` we created.

To run Jasmine specs with JsTestDriver, we need to use `jasmine-jstd-adapter`, which is hosted on GitHub at `https://github.com/ibolmo/jasmine-jstd-adapter`. This adapter works for Jasmine 1.1.x versions. Support for newer versions for example. 2.x is not yet provided by Jasmine JSTD adapter. After downloading the adapter, put the `JasmineAdapter.js` file in the `lib` directory.

We need to modify the `jsTestDriver.conf` file to add Jasmine and adapter JavaScript files:

```
server: http://localhost:9880

load:
  - lib/jasmine-1.1.0/jasmine.js
  - lib/adapter/JasmineAdapter.js
  - lib/jquery.1.11.3.min.js
  - src/*.js

test:
  - src-test/*.js
```

Recall the `Employee` object we created in *Chapter 4, Jasmine*. Let's copy the `employee.js` file to our source directory `src` and create an `employee-specs.js` file in the `src-test` directory. We need to write some specs for the `Employee` object in this file to test.

```
describe("Jasmine Spy", function() {
    it("Spying employee", function(){
        var alice = new Employee("Alice", 4, "Testing");
        spyOn(alice, "calculateSalary");
        console.log(alice.printDetails());
        expect(alice.calculateSalary).toHaveBeenCalled();
    });
```

```
it("Spying employee with arguments", function(){
    var alice = new Employee("Alice", 4, "Testing");
    spyOn(alice, "calculateSalary");
    expect(alice.calculateSalary).not.toHaveBeenCalledWith(5);
    var salary = alice.getSalary();
    console.log(salary);
});
});
```

Everything is added, now let's run our app again. You should be able to see the success messages in the output:

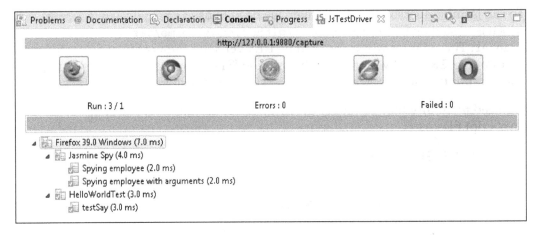

Code coverage

It's always a good practice to know about code coverage in your project. In very simple words, code coverage can be thought as the code which is tested. A higher code coverage means that the code written is carefully tested and leads to a minimal chance of occurrence of bugs. A code with the lower coverage can lead to frequent bugs since it was not properly tested.

JsTestDriver has coverage plugin available to generate a report for your project. In the `jsTestDriver.conf` file, we need to add coverage plugin to generate the report:

```
server: http://localhost:9880

load:
  - lib/jasmine-1.1.0/jasmine.js
  - lib/adapter/JasmineAdapter.js
```

```
    - lib/jquery.1.11.3.min.js
    - src/*.js

test:
    - src-test/*.js

plugin:
    - name: "coverage"
      jar: "lib/coverage-1.3.5.jar"
      module: "com.google.jstestdriver.coverage.CoverageModule"
```

After this, we also need to specify the output directory using the `--testOutput` flag. If we choose `D:/HelloWorldAppOutput` as output directory, then our command to run tests would be:

```
java -jar JsTestDriver-1.3.5.jar --tests all --testOutput d:\
HelloWorldAppOutputDirectory
```

This will create two types of files in the output directory. The first one is a `.dat` file—`jsTestDriver.conf-coverage.dat`—and second type is `.xml` files one for each browser each test. For example, output of the previous command will generate these files in the output directory:

```
jsTestDriver.conf-coverage.dat
TEST-Chrome_4302357130_Windows.AsynchronousTest.xml
TEST-Chrome_4302357130_Windows.HelloWorldTest.xml
TEST-Chrome_4302357130_Windows.JasmineaSpy.xml
TEST-Chrome_4302357130_Windows.QueueTest.xml
TEST-Firefox_390_Windows.AsynchronousTest.xml
TEST-Firefox_390_Windows.HelloWorldTest.xml
TEST-Firefox_390_Windows.JasmineaSpy.xml
TEST-Firefox_390_Windows.QueueTest.xml
```

After running tests, we can use `genhtml` to generate HTML for our coverage report. To install the `genhtml` command on Windows, we need to install `perl` and `lcov`. Cygwin is a very good option here to provide a Linux-like environment for Windows, which can be downloaded and installed from `https://cygwin.com/install.html`.

lcov can be downloaded from `https://github.com/linux-test-project/lcov/` at GitHub. Once we have the `make` utility and `perl` installed on Cygwin, just run `make install` in the `lcov` directory to install lcov. After Cygwin is installed, open terminal by navigating to **Start | All Programs | Cygwin | Cygwin Terminal**. Run the following command to create HTML reports for coverage:

```
genhtml /path-to-output-dir/jsTestDriver.conf-coverage.dat -o /path-to-
output-dir/html
```

After running the command, a number of files created for the coverage report will be generated in `/path-to-output-dir/html`. These files will include the coverage report for JavaScript files, CSS, JS, and so on.

LCOV - code coverage report

		Hit	Total	Coverage
Current view:	top level			
Test:	jsTestDriver.conf-coverage.dat	**Lines:** 709	1233	**57.5 %**
Date:	2015-07-11 12:16:22	**Functions:** 0	0	-

Directory	Line Coverage ⬦			Functions ⬦	
lib		33.3 %	1 / 3	-	0 / 0
lib/adapter		64.8 %	59 / 91	-	0 / 0
lib/jasmine-1.1.0		54.6 %	578 / 1058	-	0 / 0
src		77.3 %	34 / 44	-	0 / 0
src-test		100.0 %	37 / 37	-	0 / 0

Generated by: LCOV version 1.0

As we can see, it will show coverage in number of lines and in percentage. If you do not use the `--testOutput` flag in the command, all the output will be generated in command line. It will look as follows:

```
Total 10 tests (Passed: 10; Fails: 0; Errors: 0) (12603.00 ms)
  Firefox 39.0 Windows: Run 6 tests (Passed: 5; Fails: 0; Errors 0)
(8039.00 ms)
  Chrome 43.0.2357.130 Windows: Run 6 tests (Passed: 5; Fails: 0; Errors
0) (12603.00 ms)
D:\HelloWorldApp\.\src-test\async-test.js: 100.0% covered
D:\HelloWorldApp\.\src-test\employee-specs.js: 100.0% covered
D:\HelloWorldApp\.\src-test\helloworld-test.js: 100.0% covered
D:\HelloWorldApp\.\src-test\queue-test.js: 100.0% covered
D:\HelloWorldApp\.\lib\jasmine-1.1.0\jasmine.js: 54.631382% covered
D:\HelloWorldApp\.\lib\adapter\JasmineAdapter.js: 64.83517% covered
D:\HelloWorldApp\.\lib\jquery.1.11.3.min.js: 33.333336% covered
D:\HelloWorldApp\.\src\a-jasmine.js: 10.526316% covered
D:\HelloWorldApp\.\src\currency.js: 20.0% covered
D:\HelloWorldApp\.\src\employee.js: 84.84849% covered
D:\HelloWorldApp\.\src\helloworld.js: 83.33333% covered
```

Summary

JsTestDriver has been a very popular tool among test runners; it may not be as a great testing framework, but as a test runner it has always attracted the developers. The main reason which attracts developers can be JsTestDriver's seamless integration with popular IDEs such as Eclipse, IntelliJIdea, and NetBeans. You learned how to integrate it with Eclipse and run our tests with it. You also learned about code coverage and coverage report using `lcov genhtml`. We have been seeing tools and frameworks so far, soon you will learn about more concepts used in test-driven development.

In the next chapter, you will learn about cross-browser concerns and how to deal with them in a test-driven environment.

6
Feature Detection

There are a number of tools and frameworks available for testing your application. We have seen a number of them so far. We now move to more advanced concepts, which help us get a bug-free application. In this chapter, you will learn about feature detection for major browsers. While writing a piece of code in JavaScript, a developer often faces a question—will this code work on all browsers? Or at least, on popular browsers? Intention to write cross-browser code leads to feature detection.

The following topics will be covered in this chapter:

- Understanding feature detection
- has.js
- Modernizr
- Browser detection
- Feature testing with Modernizr
- Undetectable features

Understanding feature detection

Days are gone when there were simple JavaScript codes utilizing limited browser features, and a website would not be very complex. These days, a developer needs canvas, audio and video, geographic location of the user, drag and drop, and many more features to implement all needed requirements. Unfortunately, not all browsers support all of these features in their latest versions.

In case a feature is not supported, a developer writes a cross-browser script, which either first detects a browser or if a feature is present, and then executes suitable code for that browser. This task is very challenging as detecting a browser is not always reliable. You detect a browser, and then make an assumption that the feature will be present, which might not always be correct. An older version of browser may not support a feature or a newer version may drop a feature. You will learn about browser detection and why it is not a good practice later in this chapter.

The other way, feature detection, is what a developer needs to correctly determine whether a feature is present in the browser or not, and then make a correct decision. This will never be dependent on browser or its version. Straight and clear. For example, if canvas is available use it, otherwise do the task differently.

Available methods and libraries

There are several JavaScript libraries, which can help you detect features and browsers. Each of these libraries contains tests to detect whether the browser has support for a particular feature or not. Let's take an example of a media site, which showcases featured news videos on the website. We will use jQuery for our DOM manipulations. The following code checks if the video HTML tag is supported or not:

```
<script>
  $(document).ready(function(){
    var videoElement = "";
    videoElement = document.createElement('video');
    if(videoElement = = = undefined){
      // load via flash or something else
      $("#result").html("Video is not supported, use Flash
      or something else.");
    }else{
      //  video is supported by the browser and can play it.
      $("#result").html("Video is supported");
      $("body").append(videoElement);
      }
    });
</script>
```

In this code, we tried to create a video element and then added it to body. If a video element is created and not undefined, then the developer can use the video tag to play a video; otherwise, the developer needs to find another way to display the content. This is a very simple way of checking whether a feature is present and supported by a browser.

While every feature can be tested and detected, sometimes it may be difficult or time consuming to detect features. Therefore, there are several libraries present to help developers. **Modernizr** is the most popular feature-detection library, which is lightweight and takes very less time to perform tests. Other libraries are jQuery support and **has.js** (https://github.com/phiggins42/has.js), but these are considered to be deprecated or outdated.

has.js

has.js tests are very simple to perform and use `has('feature')` like syntax and return a Boolean value. The code in the previous example could be written as:

```
<script>
    var videoElement = "";
    $(document).ready(function(){
    if(has("video")){
        //  video is supported by the browser and can play it.
        $("#result").html("Video is supported");
        videoElement = document.createElement('video');
        $("body").append(videoElement);
    }else{
        // load via flash or something else
        $("#result").html("Video is not supported, use Flash or
        something else.");
    }
});
</script>
```

In this case, `has("video")` will return a Boolean value to help developer make a decision. Sometimes features are partially supported. To understand this, let's take the same example of displaying video content. We can check if a video tag is supported or not, but this is not sufficient as we might need to play a certain format like Ogg, Mp4, MKV, and so on. We need to further test something like this:

```
<script>
    var videoElement = "";
    $(document).ready(function(){
    if(has("video") && video.canPlayType('video/ogg;
codecs="theora, vorbis"')){
        //  video is supported by the browser and can play it.
        $("#result").html("Video is supported");
        videoElement = document.createElement('video');
        $("body").append(videoElement);
    }else{
```

```
            // load via flash or something else
            $("#result").html("Video is not supported, use Flash or
            something else.");
        }
    });
    </script>
```

Now, our code will check if it can play video type Ogg. Ogg (`https://en.wikipedia.org/wiki/Ogg`) is an open container, free video format, which is not restricted by any software patent.

Writing custom tests

Often, these libraries also provide a way to add your own tests. For example, if you want to add a test for checking drag and drop, a test skeleton using has.js would be:

```
has.add("drag-and-drop-test", function(){
var isDragAndDrop = false;
// code to check if drag and drop is supported.
    return isDragAndDrop ;
});
```

This will add a test for `drag-and-drop-test` in has.js, and we will be able to test it using `has("drag-and-drop-test")`. The function should always return a Boolean value. Similar to this, we can add tests for other libraries. You will learn to add tests for Modernizr later in the chapter.

Modernizr

Modernizr is an awesome JavaScript library for feature detection. It is great for detecting HTML5 and CSS3 features and is used widely. We are going to focus on Modernizr for feature detection in this chapter.

Downloading and setting up Modernizr

At the time of writing, Modernizr, Version 3, is the most stable version. Modernizr can be downloaded as two versions—development and production. Source code of Modernizr can be checked out from `https://github.com/Modernizr/Modernizr` at GitHub.

For the production version, Modernizr provides a custom build tool, which allows us to select only those features that we want to test. These features are divided into several sections such as CSS3, HTML5 features, and Modernizr methods and properties under options. There are almost 240+ options that are available to choose to build one consolidate file. Build tool is available at `http://modernizr.com/download/`.

Development version can be downloaded using the link `https://modernizr.com/download?do_not_use_in_production`.

Both production and development build links open the same page as seen in the following screenshot:

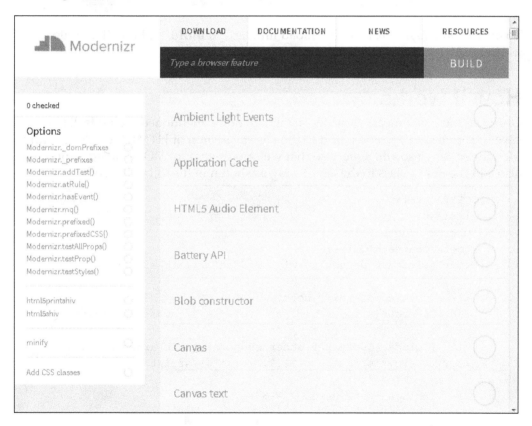

Once the required features are selected, click on the **BUILD** button and a popup, as seen in following screenshot, will appear, which will allow you to save different configuration files that can be used in the projects:

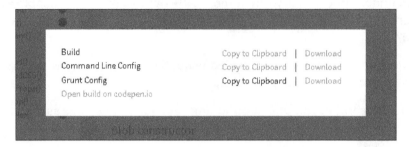

To download a JS file click on download link next to **Build**, and it will download the `modernizr-custom.js` file with selected options.

How it works

Once you have downloaded the file using any of the mentioned methods, let's save it as `modenizr.js` and add it to the `<head>` section of HTML file. Along with Modernizr, let's also add jQuery so that we can use that for DOM manipulation. We also add the `no-js` class to the `<html>` tag as shown in the following code:

```
<!DOCTYPE html>
<html class='no-js'>
    <head>
    <meta charset="utf-8">
    <title>Feature Detection with Modernizr</title>

    <!-- include modernizr here... -->
    <script src="js/modernizr.js" type="text/javascript"></script>

    <!-- include jQuery and other supporting libraries here... -->
    <script src="js/jquery.1.11.3.min.js"></script>

    <!-- include tests here... -->

    </head>

    <body>
    </body>
</html>
```

The preceding code will just load the Modenizr and jQuery libraries to the page. We added the `no-js` class to our `<html>` tag, but when Modernizr is loaded, it will add many other classes. It will also change the `no-js` class to `js`. If you inspect the code in the `<html>` tag in the browser, you will see a number of classes added as follows:

```
js flexbox flexboxlegacy canvas canvastext webgl no-touch
geolocation postmessage no-websqldatabase indexeddb hashchange
history draganddrop websockets rgba hsla multiplebgs
backgroundsize borderimage borderradius boxshadow textshadow
opacity cssanimations csscolumns cssgradients no-cssreflections
csstransforms csstransforms3d csstransitions fontface
generatedcontent video audio localstorage sessionstorage
webworkers applicationcache svg inlinesvg smil svgclippaths
```

These classes clearly tell us about supported and unsupported features. Classes starting with `no-xx`, state that feature xx is not supported by this browser (highlighted classes in the preceding listing).

Modernizr creates an object named `Modernizr` to the document, which contains all of the test results as Boolean properties. We can write a simple script to list all supported and unsupported features:

```
$(document).ready(function(){
    for(var key in Modernizr) {
        if(typeof Modernizr[key] == 'boolean'){
            console.log(key + "::" + Modernizr[key] );
            if(Modernizr[key]){
                $("#supported-
                features").append("<b>"+key+"</b><br/>");
            }else{
                $("#unsupported-
                features").append("<b>"+key+"</b><br/>");
            }
        }
    }
});
```

The preceding code will loop through the `Modernizr` object and list all the features to the browser's console. Just for listing purpose, we have also put them to elements with IDs: `supported-features` and `unsupported-features`. Running the file in different browsers will give a different list of features.

Using Modernizr

So now, we have information about available and missing features of the browser. The question being, how to make use of this information? Let's take a very simple scenario. We need to provide a border image to all the blocks. But in older version of browsers, we cannot add a border image. In a modern and updated browser, we will have `borderimage` added by Modernizr. For older browsers, where border image is not supported, a `no-borderimage` class will be added to the `<html>` tag. Along with this, we have the `.site-block` class added to each of our block. Our CSS will look as follows:

```css
.site-block {
}
/* for browsers with no support of border image */
.no-borderimage .site-block{
}
```

You will learn more about testing with Modernizr later in this chapter.

Polyfills

The term **polyfill** is given by Remy Sharp who was actually looking for a word that meant "replicate an API using JavaScript (or Flash or whatever), if the browser doesn't have it natively." Remy describes it at `https://remysharp.com/2010/10/08/what-is-a-polyfill`.

There are features which are not supported by old browsers and sometimes few new browsers as well. These are native features, which a developer might expect to exist natively, but they don't exist. That's why we need polyfills. A polyfill is a piece of code, which provides the missing feature(s) to a browser.

For example, canvas is supported by most modern browsers, but Internet Explorer versions below 9 do not support canvas. There are many polyfills available for canvas such as, FlashCanvas, excanvas, canvas-text, and many more. A developer can make use of polyfills available for canvas. Similar to canvas, there are many more features for which polyfills are created. A comprehensive list of polyfills is maintained by Modernizr at GitHub: `https://github.com/Modernizr/Modernizr/wiki/HTML5-Cross-Browser-Polyfills`.

Loading polyfills

When there are some features missing in a browser and we would want to provide those features using polyfills or an alternative to that feature, `Modernizr.load()` can test if a certain feature is supported or not and load the appropriate JavaScript based on the result. `Modernizr.load()` is not provided in the `modernizr.js` file by default and was a part of Modernizr Version 2.8.3.

`Modernizr.load()` is actually **yepnope.js** (http://yepnopejs.com/). yepnope.js was known as a conditional loader for polyfills, but now its deprecated after version 1.5.

To understand this, let's take a simple example as shown:

```
<script>
    Modernizr.load({
    test: Modernizr.touch,
    yep : 'js/touch.js',
    nope: 'js/no-touch.js'
    });
</script>
```

The preceding code will check if `touch` is available in the browser. If it is, it will load `touch.js`, otherwise it will load the `no-touch.js` file into the browser.

For the newer versions of Modernizr, we can include yepnope.js to use `Modernizr.load()`.

There are many other libraries that can load resources like RequireJS, HeadJS, and so on. The code in the previous example can also be written as follows:

```
<script>
if(Modernizr.touch){
    require(['js/touch'], function() {
    //code to execute when touch..js is loaded
        });
}else{
    require(['js/no-touch'], function() {
    //code to execute when our polyfill is loaded
        });
}
</script>
```

Similarly, other libraries can also be utilized. This helps to load only required libraries to the page, and hence save the bandwidth and make a website faster.

Supported browsers

Just like any other JavaScript library, Modernizr has a list of browsers and their supported versions. The following table shows the list:

Desktop browsers	Mobile browsers
Internet Explorer 6+	iOS mobile Safari
Mozilla Firefox 3.5+	Android webkit browser
Opera 9.6+	Opera mobile
Safari 2+	Firefox mobile
Chrome	Blackberry 6+

The preceding list covers almost all major and popular browsers.

Browser detection

An ideal way to develop a system is to perform capability testing first. We should get the information if the environment where the system will run is capable of doing things we want to do. But that hardly happens, and at the same time it is not always possible, be it any reason—unforeseen issues, changing requirements, insufficient time, and many more. That's one big reason we need browser detection and perform quick fixes.

User agent sniffing

Browser detection is mostly done by checking user agent string, which is not completely reliable because user agent string can be spoofed. A developer is encouraged to use feature detection over browser detection. You should not rely on browser detection to assume that a feature will be available, instead perform feature detection and write code accordingly.

Mostly, browsers have been sharing similar user agent strings and hence the history of user agent strings have been very dramatic. You would find more details about this at `http://webaim.org/blog/user-agent-string-history/`. The link will also help you understand why user agent sniffing is mostly unreliable.

Though a developer should not rely on browser detection using user agent string, yet here is a simple way to detect a browser. We can use navigator `userAgent` to get user agent string and then check the browser.

```
if(navigator.userAgent.indexOf("Firefox") != -1 ) {
// This browser is Firefox
}
```

Similarly, we could check for "firefox" for Mozilla Firefox, "MSIE" for Microsoft Internet Explorer (not Edge version), and so on. Look at the following user agent strings:

Browser	User agent strings
Firefox	Mozilla/5.0 (Windows NT 6.1; WOW64; rv:39.0) Gecko/20100101 Firefox/39.0
Chrome	Mozilla/5.0 (Windows NT 6.1; WOW64) AppleWebKit/537.36 (KHTML, like Gecko) Chrome/43.0.2357.130 Safari/537.36
Safari	Mozilla/5.0 (Windows; U; Windows NT 6.1; en-US) AppleWebKit/533.20.25 (KHTML, like Gecko) Version/5.0.4 Safari/533.20.27
IE 10	Mozilla/5.0 (compatible; MSIE 10.0; Windows NT 6.1; WOW64; Trident/7.0; SLCC2; .NET CLR 2.0.50727; .NET CLR 3.5.30729; .NET CLR 3.0.30729; Media Center PC 6.0; .NET4.0C; .NET4.0E)
IE 10	Mozilla/5.0 (compatible; MSIE 10.0; Windows NT 6.2; Trident/6.0)
IE 8	Mozilla/4.0 (compatible; MSIE 8.0; Windows NT 6.1; Trident/4.0)
Opera	Mozilla/5.0 (Windows NT 6.1; WOW64) AppleWebKit/537.36 (KHTML, like Gecko) Chrome/33.0.1750.58 Safari/537.36 OPR/20.0.1387.30 (Edition Next)

If you take a closer look at the user agent strings, you will know a good reason to avoid using this method for browser detection. Even if you need to use it, you should be careful. User agent string of chrome has both "chrome" and "safari", Safari has only "safari", Opera has "chrome" and "safari" both. It can be confusing to use the preceding method we discussed.

A better method is the following:

```
function detectMyBrowser(){
    var currentBrowser = "";
    if( navigator.userAgent.indexOf('Chrome') != -1 ){
        currentBrowser = 'Chrome';
    }
    if( navigator.userAgent.indexOf('MSIE') != -1 ){
        currentBrowser = 'Internet Explorer';
```

```
    }
    if( navigator.userAgent.indexOf('Firefox') != -1 ){
        currentBrowser = 'Firefox';
    }
    if( navigator.userAgent.indexOf('Safari') != -1 &&
        navigator.userAgent.indexOf('Chrome') == -1){
        currentBrowser = 'Safari';
    }
    if( navigator.userAgent.indexOf('OPR') != -1 ){
        currentBrowser = 'Opera';
    }
    console.log(currentBrowser);
    return currentBrowser;
    }
```

The preceding method will correctly work for browsers except Microsoft Internet Explorer Edge version.

Apart from creating your own method or using it, you can also use existing JavaScript libraries for browser detection such as the jQuery browser (http://api.jquery.com/jquery.browser).

Object detection

Each browser has some unique properties or functions or objects supported by it. We can use these objects to roughly determine the type of browser. For example, window.createPopup is supported by only Internet Explorer Version 5.5+ (excluding Edge version). In all other browsers, it will be undefined. So, we can use something as follows:

```
if( typeof window.createPopup !== 'undefined' ){
    currentBrowser = 'Internet Explorer';
}
```

There can be so many ways to detect a browser using object detection.

This method is more useful when it is used to detect objects and works accordingly to avoid errors. A very popular use of this is to detect the way to make AJAX work in the browser.

```
var xmlhttp;
if (window.XMLHttpRequest){
    xmlhttp=new XMLHttpRequest();
}else{
    xmlhttp=new ActiveXObject("Microsoft.XMLHTTP");
}
```

The `XMLHttpRequest` object is not supported by Internet Explorer versions below 7 so we needed to use `ActiveXObject` to make an AJAX request.

Features testing with Modernizr

There is a good number of tests written by Modernizr for feature detection. These tests by Modernizr can be classified into categories—CSS features, HTML5 features, and some features, which do not fall in these categories. In the subsections, you will learn about these features and the facility that Modernizr provides for feature testing. The following sections list a very small list of features detected by Modernizr. For a complete list, please see *Appendix, List of Features Detected by Modernizr 3*.

CSS features

For a feature, Modernizr adds a CSS class to the `<html>` element as we have seen earlier. Modernizr also adds a property to Modernizr JavaScript object for the feature. We can utilize these classes to check if a feature is present or not. The following table shows the list of few features and their respective CSS classes or JavaScript properties added by Modernizr:

Features	JavaScript properties / CSS classes	Features	JavaScript properties / CSS classes
CSS subpixel fonts	`subpixelfont`	CSS text-overflow ellipsis	`ellipsis`
CSS supports	`supports`	CSS.escape()	`cssescape`
CSS :target pseudo-class	`target`	CSS Font ex Units	`cssexunit`
CSS text-align-last	`textalignlast`	CSS Filters	`cssfilters`
CSS textshadow	`textshadow`	@font-face	`fontface`
CSS Transforms	`csstransforms`	CSS Generated Content	`generatedcontent`
CSS Transitions	`csstransitions`	CSS Gradients	`cssgradients`
CSS wrap-flow	`wrapflow`	CSS Media Queries	`mediaqueries`
CSS Animations	`cssanimations`	CSS Multiple Backgrounds	`multiplebgs`
Background position XY	`bgpositionxy`	CSS :nth-child pseudo-selector	`nthchild`
Background repeat	`bgrepeatspace`, `bgrepeatround`	CSS Object Fit	`objectfit`
Background size	`backgroundsize`	CSS Opacity	`opacity`

Features	JavaScript properties / CSS classes	Features	JavaScript properties / CSS classes
Background size cover	`bgsizecover`	CSS Overflow Scrolling	`overflowscrolling`
Border image	`borderimage`	CSS Pointer Events	`csspointerevents`
Border radius	`borderradius`	CSS position: sticky	`csspositionsticky`
Box shadow	`boxshadow`	CSS Generated Content Animations	`csspseudoanima tions`
Box sizing	`boxsizing`	CSS Generated Content Transitions	`csspseudotransi tions`
CSS calc	`csscalc`	CSS Reflections	`cssreflections`
CSS :checked pseudo-selector	`checked`	CSS Regions	`regions`
CSS font ch units	`csschunit`	CSS Font rem Units	`cssremunit`
CSS columns	`csscolumns`	CSS UI Resize	`cssresize`
CSS cubic bezier range	`cubicbezierrange`	CSS rgba	`rgba`
CSS display run-in	`display-runin`	CSS Stylable Scrollbars	`cssscrollbar`
CSS display table	`displaytable`	CSS Shapes	`shapes`

Let's understand how to use these properties.

Take an example where we need to set the background size to half of the screen, that is 50 percent, but this will fail on IE below 9 because of no support for background size. Modernizr will add `no-backgroundsize` to IE below version 9 and will add `backgroundsize` to supporting browsers. In this case, we can add our CSS as follows:

```
.box-bg{
width: 400px;
    height: 100px;
    padding: 10px;
    border: 1px solid #cecece;
    background: url(images/background-image-tree.jpg);
    background-size: 50%;
    background-repeat:  no-repeat;
    }
    .no-backgroundsize .box-bg{
    background: url(images/background-image-cloud.jpg);
    }
```

We have the `.box-bg` CSS class for browsers supporting background size and for the other browsers we added a fallback with CSS class `.no-backgroundsize` and assigned a different image for background. In case we want to modify background for these browsers using JavaScript, we could use the `Modernizr.backgroundsize` property to test if the `background-size` property is supported:

```
$(document).ready(function(){
    if( ! Modernizr.backgroundsize){
    $(".box-bg").css("background-image", "url(images/background-
    image-cloud.jpg)");
    }
});
```

HTML5 features

Similar to CSS properties, Modernizr adds classes and properties to the JavaScript object. The list of few features is provided in the following table:

Features	Modernizr CSS classes or JS properties
applicationCache	applicationcache
Canvas	canvas
Canvas text	canvastext
Drag and drop	draganddrop
hashchange event	hashchange
History management	history
HTML5 audio	audio
HTML5 video	video
IndexedDB	indexeddb
localStorage	localstorage
Cross-window messaging	postmessage
sessionStorage	sessionstorage
Web sockets	websockets
Web SQL database	websqldatabase
Web worker	webworkers

Modernizr also detects available HTML5 input attributes and input types. It will add the following properties to the `Modernizr` object:

- `Modernizr.input.autocomplete`
- `Modernizr.input.autofocus`
- `Modernizr.input.list`
- `Modernizr.input.max`
- `Modernizr.input.min`
- `Modernizr.input.multiple`
- `Modernizr.input.pattern`
- `Modernizr.input.placeholder`
- `Modernizr.input.required`
- `Modernizr.input.step`

All the preceding subproperties are Boolean in value. All of these properties return true for the latest version of Firefox, Chrome, IE version greater than 9. Similarly, there are input types:

- `Modernizr.inputtypes.color` // false on IE
- `Modernizr.inputtypes.date` // false on FF, IE
- `Modernizr.inputtypes.datetime` // false on IE, FF and Chrome
- `Modernizr.inputtypes['datetime-local']` // false on FF, IE
- `Modernizr.inputtypes.email`
- `Modernizr.inputtypes.month` // false on FF, IE
- `Modernizr.inputtypes.number` // false on FF, IE and Chrome
- `Modernizr.inputtypes.range`
- `Modernizr.inputtypes.search`
- `Modernizr.inputtypes.tel`
- `Modernizr.inputtypes.time` // false on FF, IE
- `Modernizr.inputtypes.url`
- `Modernizr.inputtypes.week` // false on FF, IE

Most of the input types are yet to be implemented by major browsers, hence there are many subproperties that return false.

With the help of these properties, you can test if a feature is present or not and then load the appropriate polyfills or achieve the functionality using alternative ways. Let's take an example of datepicker that we use in our forms to allow user to enter dates. We can use an input as follows:

```
<input type="date" name="dateOfBirth" id="dateOfBirth" />
```

However, this won't work on all browsers, so we test for input type date.

```
$(document).ready(function(){
    if(! Modernizr.inputtype.date){
    // use custom datepicker
    $("#dateOfBirth").datepicker();
    }
});
```

In the preceding code, `if` condition will be true for Firefox and Internet Explorer, and we can use datepicker for only those browsers.

Miscellaneous features

Apart from the features falling in HTML5 and CSS features categories, there are features which are environment dependent such as touch, geolocation, and so on. A list of few of the features is in the following table:

Features	Modernizr CSS classes or JS properties
Geolocation API	geolocation
Inline SVG	inlinesvg
SMIL	smil
SVG	svg
SVG clip paths	svgclippaths
Touch events	touch
WebGL	webgl

Similar to other properties, we can use these properties/CSS classes to test if a feature is supported.

For example, check WebGL:

```
if (Modernizr.webgl) {
    // WebGL is supported.
} else {
    // WebGL is not supported, use alternative ways.
}
```

Few of the preceding properties are not fully supported by Modernizr. SVG clip paths test is only for clip paths in SVG. Touch test shows if the browser supports touch events, but that does not mean that the device has touchscreen.

Plugins for additional tests

The tests we just checked out were core of Modernizr. Many more tests are also available as a form of plugin to Modernizr at GitHub (`https://github.com/Modernizr/Modernizr/tree/master/feature-detects`). The repository here has tests for all major and frequent requirements.

Modernizr methods

Modernizr allows you to extend it by writing more tests and utilizing them to detect features of your choice. Along with that, there are methods available for testing CSS prefixes and media queries.

Modernizr.prefixed()

You might have seen CSS as in the following example:

```
-moz-border-radius: 10px 10px;
-webkit-border-top-left-radius: 10px;
-webkit-border-top-right-radius: 10px;
-webkit-border-bottom-right-radius: 10px;
-webkit-border-bottom-left-radius: 10px;
border-radius: 10px 10px;
```

The preceding CSS is to put radius on elements like div and so on. If you note, there are prefixes before `border-radius` or `border-xxx-xxx-radius`. These are called **vendor** or **browser** prefixes. The following table shows the browsers and their prefixes:

Browsers	CSS prefixes
Firefox	`-moz-`
Android	`-webkit-`
Chrome	`-webkit-`
Internet Explorer	`-ms-`
iOS	`-webkit-`
Opera	`-o-`
Safari	`-webkit-`

When these prefixes are applied, a browser applies a property that it understands, and will drop the rest of the properties. To understand this further, let's see the inspect view in IE8 and Chrome:

Internet Explorer added a checkbox to the properties that it understands and underline to the properties which are not supported. Google Chrome grayed out `-moz-border-radius` and strikes through the properties that are not applied.

Mostly, we just add these prefixes to standard CSS properties as we did for `border-radius`. This may not be true always though, for example, the older version of the Chrome browser uses `-webkit-gradient` for `liner-gradient`.

Browsers use prefixes to add new features and to implement feature for which specification is not yet finalized. There are times when a developer modifies CSS styles using JavaScript. Let's see the following example which modifies the radius of `div` dynamically when clicked on. The `div` tag has ID `box-no-radius` so that the added event would be as follows:

```
$("#box-no-radius").click(function(){
this.style.webkitBorderRadius = "10px 10px"; // for chrome
});
```

Note that we are using `webkitBorderRadius`, which stands for CSS property `-webkit-border-radius` in Camel case with no spaces. But this requires one line per browser. The `Modernizr.prefixed()` method saves us from writing so much code. Let's look at the following code:

```
$("#box-no-radius").click(function(){
    this.style[Modernizr.prefixed('borderRadius')] = "10px 10px";
});
```

The preceding code will work for all browsers. All we need to provide is the CSS property in Camel case with no spaces and hyphens removed. This will work for all browsers.

In JavaScript, to access properties of an object, both square bracket notation and dot notation are permitted. `Modernizr.prefixed()` will return the correct property string for the browser.

One more variant of this method is `Modernizr.prefixed(str, obj [, scope])`, using which we can find prefix DOM properties and methods. This method looks for a specific property `str` in given object `obj` in DOM.

```
Modernizr.prefixed('getUserMedia', navigator)  // returns function
Modernizr.prefixed('performance', window) // returns function
```

The first call will look for `getUserMedia` in navigator object in DOM. For Firefox, it returns the `mozGetUserMedia()` function. The second call will look for performance in the `window` object. If the specified property is not a function, it will return the value it finds. This value can be an object, Boolean, number, and so on.

If a function is found, it will be bound to what we provide in the second argument. We can provide a third argument (scope) to which it should be bound.

```
var matchesSelectorFn = Modernizr.prefixed("matchesSelector",
HTMLElement.prototype, document.body);
matchesSelectorFn("body") // returns true
```

`Modernizr.prefixed('getUserMedia', navigator)` will return the function, but if you want this call to return just the name of the function, then pass the `false` as third argument.

```
Modernizr.prefixed('getUserMedia', navigator, false)
```

This will return the `mozGetUserMedia` string on Firefox, `webkitGetUserMedia` on Google Chrome.

Modernizr.prefixedCSS()

This function returns the prefixed CSS property with hyphens. This is helpful for testing HTML elements `HTMLElement`, since it can return only CSS properties.

```
Modernizr.prefixedCSS("binding")   //returns -moz-binding on
firefox.
```

The syntax of the CSS property can be hyphens or Camel case. `Modernizr.prefixedCSS("column-width")` or `Modernizr.prefixedCSS("columnWidth")` both are same calls.

```
Modernizr.prefixedCSS("columnWidth")
// returns -webkit-column-width on chrome.
// returns -moz-column-width on Firefox.
```

Modernizr.mq()

Another method is `Modernizr.mq()`, which examines media query. This method tests the media query against the current state of the window.

Syntax: `Modernizr.mq(str)`

The argument `str` is a media query.

To test if a browser supports media query or not. This will return true or false.

```
Modernizr.mq('only all');
```

For a responsive website, we can check:

```
Modernizr.load([
  {
    // The test: Check if browser understands media queries
    test : Modernizr.mq('only all'),
    // If it doesn't, then load alternative solutions e.g.
    respond.js
```

```
        nope : '/js/respond.js'
    }
]);
```

To test if `min-width` is supported in media query:

```
Modernizr.mq('(min-width: 0px)')
```

Modernizr.on()

This method checks for a feature and passes the result as an argument to a function which is a second argument to the `Modernizr.on()` function:

```
Modernizr.on('webgl', function( result ) {
    if (result) {
        // the browser has webgl
        console.log("WebGL is present");
    } else {
        // the browser does not have webgl
        console.log("WebGL is not present");
    }
});
```

If you note the preceding code, Modernizr will check if WebGL support is present in the browser and pass the result to a function in which a user can make a decision.

Modernizr.atRule()

This method is similar to `Modernizr.on()`. This method tests a given rule in the `window.CSSRule` object in the browser.

```
$(document).ready(function(){
var isMediaSupported = Modernizr.atRule("@media");
    if (isMediaSupported) {
        console.log("Media is supported");
    } else {
        console.log("Media is not present");
    }
}
});
```

The preceding code checks if media is supported in the browser or not and uses that to make a decision.

Modernizr.addTest()

Sometimes when Modernizr has no tests to cover your case, you can write your own tests using the `Modernizr.addTest()` function. This function is for variants:

```
Modernizr.addTest(str, fn)
Modernizr.addTest(str, bool)
Modernizr.addTest({str: fn, str2: fn2})
Modernizr.addTest({str: bool, str2: fn})
```

Suppose we want to test for a new feature, which Modernizr still does not support. Let's call this `newFeature`, and then we write a test:

```
Modernizr.addTest('newFeature', function(){
  var isNewFeaturePresent = false;
  // code to test if new feature is present
  return isNewFeaturePresent;
});
```

Now if a browser supports `newFeature`, Modernizr will add a `newfeature` class to HTML element otherwise it will add a `no-newfeature` class. If you add the code to a script element and run the code in the browser, you will see the `no-newfeature` class added. The following screenshot is of Firebug in Firefox. The `no-newfeature` CSS class will be present because in our implementation we just returned `false`:

Similar to this, we can add a support for testing new features. One point to note is that the feature test name should be without dashes. For example, `new-feature` is not recommended and `newfeature` or `newFeature` should be used.

Modernizr.testStyles()

This method has the following signature:

```
Modernizr.testStyles(str,fn[, nodes, testnames])
```

With this method, we can add some styles to document and then test an element. This test injects an element with ID `modernizr`. Let's checkout the following example:

```
$(document).ready(function(){
    Modernizr.testStyles('#modernizr { width: 100px; color: blue;
                          }', function(elem, rule){
console.log(elem);
Modernizr.addTest('width', elem.offsetWidth == 100);
    });
});
```

This will inject an element to the document as follows:

```
<div id="modernizr">
<style id="smodernizr">
    #modernizr { width: 100px; color: blue; }
</style>
</div>
```

It will perform width added by `Modernizr.addTest()` on this element. Accordingly, it will add a CSS class `width` or `no-width` to the HTML element.

In case you want to perform tests on multiple elements you can use `nodes` argument of the function. Nodes is a number specifying the number of elements that will be injected. By default, IDs of those elements will be `modernizr[n]` where n is the number. See the following example:

```
Modernizr.testStyles('#modernizr { width: 100px; color: blue; }',
function(elem, rule){
Modernizr.addTest('width', elem.offsetWidth == 100);
}, 2);
```

We have specified 2 for nodes argument, which will add two elements with IDs `modernizr1` and `modernizr2` by default:

```
<div id="modernizr">
<div id="modernizr2"></div>
<div id="modernizr1"></div>
<style id="smodernizr">
    #modernizr { width: 100px; color: blue; }
</style>
</div>
```

If we want to provide specific IDs, we can use `testnames` argument, which will take an array of string that will be IDs of those elements. If we provide `["video", "image"]` as in the following example, the elements with ID video and image will be created and added into the document.

```
Modernizr.testStyles('#modernizr { width: 100px; color: blue; }',
function(elem, rule){
Modernizr.addTest('width', elem.offsetWidth == 100);
}, 2, ["video", "image"]);
```

Modernizr.testProp()

This method takes one argument to check if the specified property is recognized:

```
Modernizr.testProp(str)
```

We must provide the property name in Camel case as in the following example:

```
Modernizr.testProp('pointerEvents')
```

This will return `true` on the latest version of browsers—FF, Chrome IE, and so on—and will return `false` on IE versions below 9.

Modernizr.testAllProps()

This method takes one argument to check if the specified property or its vendor prefixed variant is recognized.

```
Modernizr.testAllProps(str)
```

We must provide the property name in Camel case as in the following example:

```
Modernizr.testAllProps('borderRadius')
```

This method returns `true` or `false`. This will return `false` for IE version below 9 and `true` on latest versions of Firefox, Chrome, IE, and so on.

Modernizr.hasEvent()

This method has the following signature, which takes one argument as string that is the event name and an optional argument as element to test on.

```
Modernizr.hasEvent(str [,elem])
```

This method will detect if the browser supports the event or not. For example, the following code will return `false` on desktops such as Firefox, Chrome browser, and so on.

```
Modernizr.hasEvent('gesturestart')
```

Modernizr._prefixes and Modernizr._domPrefixes

`Modernizr._prefixes` and `Modernizr._domPrefixes` are JavaScript arrays, which are holding browser prefixes for both CSS and DOM properties.

Variables	Values
Modernizr._prefixes	["", "-webkit-", "-moz-", "-o-", "-ms-", ""]
Modernizr._domPrefixes	["webkit", "moz", "o", "ms"]

We can use these properties along with join to get all vendor prefixed properties to test against. For example, if we need to test CSS `calc()`, we can do so using the following code:

```
<script>
$(document).ready(function(){
    Modernizr.addTest('testcsscalc', function() {
        var prop = 'width:';
        var value = 'calc(5px);';
        var elementDiv = document.createElement('div');
        elementDiv.style.cssText = prop +
        Modernizr._prefixes.join(value + prop);

        return !!elementDiv.style.length;
    });
});
</script>
```

The preceding code will result in CSS class `testcsscalc` or `no-testcsscalc` added to the HTML element. Here, `prop + Modernizr._prefixes.join(value + prop)` will try to add the following CSS styles:

```
width:calc(5px);
width:-webkit-calc(5px);
width:-moz-calc(5px);
```

```
width:-o-calc(5px);
width:-ms-calc(5px);
width:  // blank is added in case no other property is supported.
```

The browser will take the supported CSS style and apply it to `elementDiv`. For example Firefox 35, Chrome, and Internet Explorer greater than 8 will use `calc(5px)` for width.

Similar to this, we can use `Modernizr._domPrefixes` with join, which will return browser prefixed DOM properties. For example `'prop:value; ' + Modernizr._domPrefixes.join('Prop' + ':value; ') + ':value'` will return DOM properties as `prop:value; webkitProp:value; mozProp:value; oProp:value; ms:value`.

Undetectable features

When there is not sufficient confidence that a feature exists or not, a feature is said to be undetectable. Not everything can be detected by Modernizr because of its limitations or yet to be developed or are partially supported. It is said to be relied on other ways to detect these features. One of these ways is browser detection, which we discussed in the previous section.

Undetectable features are classified into several categories such as HTML5 features that are related to audio/video, networking, typography, events, CSS, and IE Edge. The features mentioned in these categories are found to be undetectable by Modernizr. This list is maintained by Modernizr in their wiki and can be found here at GitHub `https://github.com/Modernizr/Modernizr/wiki/Undetectables()`.

Let's take an example of using `@font-face`. We are using raleway fonts available at `https://github.com/theleagueof/raleway`. If you see, all versions of IE will add the `fontface` CSS class to HTML element, but not all types of fonts are supported by IE version below 9:

```css
@font-face{
    font-family: customFontThin;
    src: url(fonts/raleway_thin-webfont.woff);
}
.box{
    width: 300px;
    height: 100px;
    padding: 10px;
    border: 1px solid #cecece;
    font-family: customFontThin;
}
```

Since IE below version 9 does not support woff fonts, this will render to default IE font family (verdata, arial, and so on).

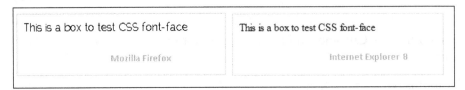

IE Version 9 and above will understand the woff font format and render correct fonts:

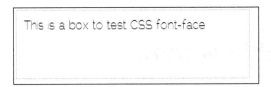

To add a fallback, you would need to rely on browser detection and add a different font or EOT font format for IE versions below 9.

Summary

Our primary objective is to write cross-browser code for our websites. In order to develop code that works on all major browsers, we need to detect support for features we are going to use. Thus, feature detection becomes a very critical part of a software development when it comes to develop a uniform UI. JavaScript libraries such as Modernizr help detecting features neatly. In this chapter, you learned how to use Modernizr to detect various CSS and HTML5 features. You learned about some useful API functions of Modernizr, which help us test features and extend Modernizr further for detecting features that are not yet supported by Modernizr.

You also learned about browser detection and feature detection and why browser detection is discouraged. On the other hand, you learned that there are still some features left which are called undetectable features.

In the next chapters, you will learn about observer pattern and its implementation to help you develop systems.

7

Observer Design Pattern

In this chapter, you will learn about the observer pattern in JavaScript. We will see its advantages, disadvantages, usage, and so on. We will see different faces of observer pattern and its use with the help of observer and subject class. We will also see how we can optimize code using the observer pattern.

Overview

The observer pattern defines a relationship between more than one object where one object is observed by many others. The system is designed in such a way that when a state of the observed object is changed, all observing objects get notified automatically. This pattern is also known as dependents and pub/sub (publication/subscription).

Mainly people like to use the observer pattern in JavaScript, and there are possibilities/chances that people are using it already. We commonly use event handling on DOM elements in all size of application and that can be achieved with the use of observer pattern.

The main and very important feature of the observer pattern is that we can add or remove the observer at runtime. The observer pattern gives an ability to subscribe to an event and then give a notification to the user when the event comes into the picture. With the use of the observer pattern user can get facility of object-oriented design and it also provides loose coupling.

Many different implementations are available in observer pattern such as event dispatcher/listener and publish/subscribe. These implementations have common ability to notify one or many objects via some sort of communication mechanism. In the observer pattern, a subject class calls an update method of observer instances, which can be one to many. Any specific details are not needed to be known to the subject class about the observer instances other than that all observers implement common interface (subject) to receive updates. Due of this behavior, we can say that it promotes loose coupling implementation.

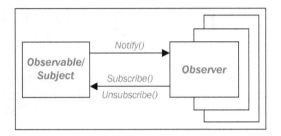

In the preceding diagram, we can see that more than one observer can subscribe or unsubscribe to observable/subject. Observable/subject will notify all the observers, which are subscribed whenever any update will be there.

Let's understand one-to-many relationship between subject and observers in the form of the class diagram. In this diagram, we will understand how observers get notified or updated in case of state change of subject:

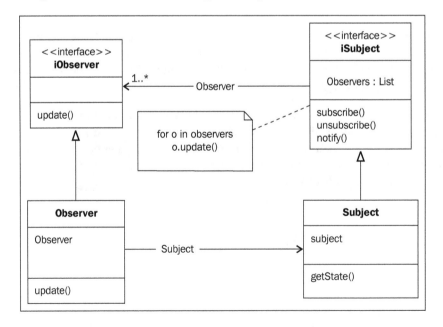

The objects involved in the preceding class diagram are:

- `iObserver`: It defines an interface that should be updated in case of state change for the subject.

- `iSubject`: It knows that how many observers are subscribed to the subject. It provides interface to subscribe and unsubscribe observer objects.

- `Subject`: It will be used to update observers, which are subscribed to it.

- `Observer`: It will maintain a reference to the `Subject` class. It will implement the `iObserver` interface, which will help to make its object consistent with the subject.

When to use it

Observer pattern is normally used in the following scenarios:

- When a change in one object should be done for an unknown number of objects

- When an action or update of one object requires an update or action change for another object

- When an object should be able to notify other objects without knowing any details about those objects

Advantages

The observer pattern helps to find out relationships between different modules in detail. As the user knows relationship of modules in detail, they can easily design subjects and observers objects. This way of designing code can help us break down modules into smaller task, which at the end turns into quality code and improve reusability of code in the system.

Next point, which encourages us to use the observer pattern, is to provide consistency between subjects and observers objects without making objects tightly coupled. For example, the `Observable` object doesn't need to worry about details of observers while notifying these objects.

We can add or remove observers at runtime, which can lead us to achieve a concept called **Hot Swapping**. This will create dynamic relationships between the subject and observers.

Disadvantages

Making loosely coupled observers and subjects can create difficulty to achieve some part of system as per the expectations. For example, Subject doesn't have more details about observers and if the system crashes suddenly, then the subject will not have way to get idea about observers due to loosely coupled system.

Due to dynamic relationship between objects, update to more than one observer can become costly sometimes when switching happens frequently.

Different implementations of the observer

The following implementations are available for the observer pattern:

- Event dispatcher/listener
- Publish/subscribe

Let's understand both the implementations in detail.

Event dispatcher/listener

The event dispatcher/listener (event emitter) implementation allows broadcasting data to more than one consumer. EventEmitter can be inherited in the case of more than one event represented by one object. We can use the on function for the EventEmitter implementation in the observer pattern to define objects for listening to an event. Objects in the event dispatcher implementation uses custom events that can be inherited from an event dispatcher object. It uses different kind of strings to identify the type of the event.

The following is the sample code for the event dispatcher/listener:

```
var EventEmitter = require("events").EventEmitter;
var eventEmitter =  new EventEmitter();
eventEmitter.on("touch",function()
{
    Console.log("Touch event has occured");
});
eventEmitter.emit("touch");
eventEmitter.once("onceExa", function ()
{
    console.log("This is executed only once");
});
eventEmitter.removeListener("onceExa");
```

As discussed here, we used the on function to define a custom event in our code. We started our example by creating an object of EventEmitter. Once we created the eventEmitter object, we used different methods such as on, emit, and once. The on method is defined with two parameters; one is the name of event on which the object will listen, and other one is the function which will be executed once that event will be called. Once the event is defined, we can fire that event with the use of the emit method.

There is one more way to fire any event. We can pass data while firing any event:

```
eventEmitter.emit("touch",objectData);
```

By default, node will allow 10 listeners. If we want to define custom limit for listener, then we can define that with the use of setMaxListeners(n) as shown:

```
eventEmitter.setMaxListeners(20);
```

The other method that we used in the example is once(). This method is normally used to call any listener only once. Let's say that we want to remove the listener after listening to it once, then we can use the removeListener() method as shown in our preceding example.

Other methods and properties available in an event emitter are as follows:

- emitter.removeAllListeners([event]): The removeAllListeners method removes all listeners of the specified event if specified. Removing listeners that were added elsewhere in the code is not a good idea (for example, sockets or file streams).

- EventEmitter.defaultMaxListeners: This property allows you to set the default number of maximum listeners for any event emitter. The emitter. setMaxListeners(n) method sets the maximum on a per-instance basis. emitter.setMaxListeners(n) has precedence over EventEmitter. defaultMaxListeners, so use emitter.defaultMaxListeners with care.

- emitter.listeners(event): It returns the list of listeners listening to the particular event.

- emitter.emit(event[, arg1][, arg2][, ...]): It executes all the listens in order with the specified arguments. It returns true if event started listening or else returns false.

- EventEmitter.listenerCount(emitter, event): It returns number of listeners that are listening to a specified event.

- Event: 'newListener': This event is emitted when any new listener has been added. Listener may not be added to array, when this event is triggered.

- Event: 'removeListener': This event is emitted when any listener has been removed. A listener may not be removed from array, when this event is triggered.

Publish/subscribe

Let's see a few of the implementations available for publisher/subscriber implementation. Next, we will understand what all roles come into the picture when we talk about publisher/subscriber implementation.

Subscriber is responsible to subscribe and unsubscribe to the publisher. They receive an update from the publisher for the change.

Publisher is responsible to update its subscribers for the change happen. They have the option of being taken from or giving an update.

Push versus pull

Let's see the example of observer pattern in real world, generally in the Internet world, users who are using e-commerce website, register themselves to sites to purchase products. Once they register, websites send notifications of offers or any kind of updates about websites to users. In this scenario, we can see that users who have registered to the e-commerce website are subscribers and e-commerce website is the publisher for us. This scenario can be called as push strategies, as the e-commerce website is pushing all the offers to users who have subscribed to sites. The other strategy is a pull strategy that can be defined as subscriber check for an update whenever needed from the publisher. In our example, when a user finds a particular product based on the need on an e-commerce website, is pull strategy for us as subscriber is going to publisher for finding the product or update about product when it is needed.

Sample code

```
var siteowner = new Observable;

var User = function(offers) {
    // offers delivered to Users
};
siteowner.subscribeUser(User);
/*
* deliver an offers/update to user of ecommerce website
```

```
* sends out the notifications to all customers.
*/
siteowner.notify('notify all about update');
/*
* User deactivate account in site
*/
siteowner.unSubscribeUser(User);
```

In this code, we have seen the publisher/subscriber model in terms of the
e-commerce website. Let's understand the API that we are using in the
observer pattern in detail to understand each step in detail.

Understanding patterns in API

We have seen what all objects are involved in the observer pattern; we will
understand those objects in the API. We need an array of users that can be
defined in the `siteowner` constructor:

```
function siteowner() {
    this.users = [];
}
```

The notify method

Site owners need an ability to notify users of sites. We can simply extend the
publisher and all `siteowner` instances required to deliver data. The `siteowner`
prototype is used to extend the `notify` method You can simply extend the
publisher prototype with a `notify` method for all user objects to share:

```
siteowner.prototype.notify = function(data) {
    this.users.forEach(
        function(msg)
    {
        msg(data);
    });
    return this;
};
```

In this method, we used `forEach` to iterate each user of the site.

Subscribe

Now, we will provide subscription ability to users with the use of the `subscribe` prototype:

```
Function.prototype.subscribe = function(siteowner) {
    siteowner.users.push(this);
    return this;
};
```

In the mentioned method, we are extending the `Function` object prototype. We are using the `subscribe` prototype to push each and every users of site to `siteowner`. Now this subscription function will be used to subscribe to the site with the use of the preceding method.

Unsubscribe

The `unsubscribe` method will be used in case any user of site wants to deactivate their account:

```
Function.prototype.unsubscribe = function(siteowner) {
    siteowner.users = siteowner.users.filter(
        function(u) {
            if ( u !== that ) {
                return u;
            }
        }
    );
    return this;
};
```

Observer with topics

Topics in the observer pattern contains more than one observable objects. Normally, it can happen that we need to create multiple observable objects in some situation. In that case, it is better that we use topic functionality of the observer pattern. Example of topics in the observer pattern is as follows:

```
var Observable = {
    users: [],
    addUser: function(item, observer) {
        this.users[item] || (this.observers[topic] = [])

        this.users[item].push(observer)
    },
```

```
removeUser: function(item, observer) {

if (!this.users[item])
    return;

  var index = this.users[item].indexOf(observer)

  if (~index) {
    this.users[item].splice(index, 1)
  }
},

  notifyUsers: function(item, note) {
  if (!this.users[item])
    return;


for (var i = this.users[item].length - 1; i >= 0; i--) {
    this.users[item][i](note)
  };
}

}

Observable.addUser('bag', function(note){
  console.log("First User note:" + note)
})

Observable.addUser('alerts', function(note){
  console.log("Second user note:" + note)
})

Observable.notifyUsers('bag', 'item in bag')

Observable.notifyUsers('alerts', 'notification to user')
```

More advanced versions may have features as follows:

- Subtopics (for example, /bar/green or bar.green)
- Publishing to topic propagates to subtopics
- Publishing to all topics
- Giving a priority to subscribers

Observer pattern using jQuery.Callbacks

Let's see an example of the observer pattern using the `jQuery.Callbacks` function.

To start with, let's add two functions which can help to understand the following flags that can be used with `jQuery.Callbacks`:

```
function newsAlert(notification) {
  alert(notification);
}
```

```
function appAlert(notification) {
  alert( "In appAlert function: "+notification);
  return false;
}
```

Possible flags available for `jQuery.callbacks` are listed as follows:

- once: It will make sure that callback is called only once.

  ```
  var messages = $.Callbacks( "once" );
  messages.add(newsAlert);
  messages.fire("First Notificaiton");
  messages.add(appAlert);
  messages.fire("Second Notification");
  ```

  Here, the output is `First Notification`.

  Whenever run for the first time, we will get `First Alert` as an output.

- memory: This flag will be used to keep track of old values and will call any of callback from the list that has been fired with the recent values:

  ```
  var messages = $.Callbacks( "memory" );
  messages.add(newsAlert);
  messages.fire("First Notification");
  messages.add(appAlert);
  messages.fire("second Notification");
  messages.remove(appAlert);
  messages.fire("Third Notification");
  ```

  Here, the output is:
  ```
  First Notification
  In App Alert: First Notification
  Second Notification
  In App Alert: Second Notification
  Third Notification
  ```

We can see in the output even though we removed `appAlert` it has been called with latest values on the screen.

- `unique`: It will make sure that callback is added only once in a list so that duplicates are not allowed in the list:

```
var messages = $.Callbacks( "unique" );
messages.add(newsAlert);
messages.fire("First Notification");
messages.add(newsAlert);
messages.add(appAlert);
messages.fire("Second Notification");
messages.remove(appAlert);
messages.fire("Third Notification");
```

Here, the output is:

```
First Notification
Second Notification
In app Alert : Second Notification
Third Notification
```

We can see that `newsAlert` is added twice in the output, but it in actual, it is added only once.

- `stopOnFalse`: It will break the callback if any `false` value occurs.

```
function newsAlert(message) {
    alert(message);
    return false;
}

function appAlert(message) {
    appAlert( "In App Alert: " + message);
    return false;
}

    var messages = $.Callbacks("stopOnFalse");
    messages.add(newsAlert);
    messages.fire("First Notification");
    messages.add(appAlert);
    messages.fire("Second Notification");
    messages.remove(appAlert);
    messages.fire("Third Notification");
```

Here, the output is:

```
First Notification
Second Notification
Third Notification
```

We can see that it has printed only `First Notification`, `Second Notification`, and `Third Notification` in the output, as both the functions are returning false, it has not called callback for those two functions.

Let's see a simple example of `jQuery.Callbacks` using the mentioned options:

```
var messages = jQuery.Callbacks()

, Item = {

    publish: messages.fire,
    subscribe: messages.add,
    unsubscribe: messages.remove
  }

function newsAlert(message){
   alert("In News Alert: " + message);
}


function appAlert(message){
   alert("In app Alert: " + message);
}


Item.subscribe(newsAlert);
Item.subscribe(appAlert);
Item.publish('First Notification');
Item.publish('Second Notification');
```

In the preceding example, we defined one object named `Item` in the callback method. Here, we assign fire event to publish, add event to subscribe, and remove to unsubscribe. With the use of the `Item` object, we are adding two subscribers using `newsAlert` and `appAlert` functions. Whenever any notification comes for `newsAlert` and `appAlert`, `First Notification` and `Second Notification` get printed on the output screen.

Implementing the observer pattern using TDD

We will see how we can use TDD to implement the observer pattern. We will use the red, green, and refactor life cycle of TDD to understand it in more detail.

Red step (code with error)

Let's try to add code, which has some dependency. Don't include dependency in the first step and see what error it's giving. Normally in the red step, we have some code with error, and then in next step we add proper code to make it green.

```
<script type="text/javascript">

Object.defineProperty(employee.status, 'Active', {
    get: function () {
        return inactive;
    },

    set: function (status) {


        Object.getNotifier(this).notify({
            type: 'update',
            name: 'Inactive',
            oldValue: inactive
        });

        // Let's also print the value in logger anytime it gets
        // set for status
        console.log('set', status);

        inactive = b;
    }
});
</script>
```

When we run the preceding code, we get the following output:

```
ReferenceError: employee is not defined
Object.defineProperty(employee.status, 'Active', {
observer-notifier.html (line 2)
```

Green step (with running code)

We have seen that in the preceding code dependency of `empModel` was not there and we used that object in code. Let's add employee as a model and make code green:

```javascript
var employee = {
    status: {},// variable label
    StatusModified: false
};
```

Let's finish the implementation by adding few proper lines:

```javascript
<script type="text/javascript">
var employee = {
    status: {},// variable status
    StatusModified: false
};


var inactive = "Active";


Object.defineProperty(employee.status, 'Active', {

    get: function () {
        return inactive;
    },
    set: function (status) {

        Object.getNotifier(this).notify({

            type: 'update',
            name: 'Inactive',
            oldValue: inactive

        });

        // Let's also print the value in logger anytime it gets
        // set for status
        console.log('set', status);

        inactive = b;
    }

});
```

```
// Which we then observe

Object.observe(employee, function(modifications) {
    modifications.forEach(function(modification, i) {
        console.log(modification);
    });

});

// Examples

employee.status = 'Employee Status';


employee.modifiedby = Date.now();

delete employee.StatusModified;

</script>
```

On running script again, we get the following output:

```
Object observer-notifier.html:43
    name: "status"
    object: Object
    oldValue: Object
    type: "update"
    __proto__: Object
Object observer-notifier.html:43
    name: "modifiedby"
    object: Object
    type: "add"
    __proto__: Object
Object observer-notifier.html:43
    name: "StatusModified"
    object: Object
    oldValue: false
    type: "delete"
    __proto__: Object
employee.status.Active = "Inactive";
"Inactive"
```

Refactoring

We have run our code properly in the green step, now let's start thinking about refactoring the code. We can think about refactoring only when we run the code in the green stage.

Let's think what we can change in our example to make it more generic:

```
<script type="text/javascript">
if(!Object.observe){
    alert('Your browser does not support Object.observe, this demo
    cannot work !');
}

var employee = {
    status: {},
    StatusModified: false
};

var inactive = "Active";


Object.defineProperty(employee.status, 'Active', {
    get: function () {
        return inactive;
    },
    set: function (status) {

        Object.getNotifier(this).notify({
            type: 'update',
            name: 'Inactive',
            oldValue: inactive
        });

        // Let's also print the value in logger anytime it gets
        // set for status

        console.log('set', status);

        inactive = b;
    }
});
```

```
function observer(modifications) {

    modifications.forEach(function(modificaiton, i) {

    console.log('what property changed? ' + modification.name);
    console.log('how did it modify? ' + modification.type);
    console.log('whats the current value? ' +
                modification.object[modification.name]);
    console.log(modification); // all changes

});

};

// Examples


employee.status = 'Employee Status';

empModel.modifiedby = Date.now();


delete employee.StatusModified;
console.log(Object.observe(employee,observer));
employee.status.Active = "active";
console.log(employee);
employee.status = "status";
console.log(employee.status);
Object.unobserve(employee,observer);
employee.status = "status changed";
console.log(empModel.status);
</script>
```

Let's see what output the refactored code is giving. The output will be printed on console as we have used `console.log`:

Object observer-refactor-code.html:83
   status: "status changed"
   updatedby: 1438754040671
   __proto__: Object

Object observer-refactor-code.html:85
   status: "status changed" updatedby: 1438754040671

```
    __proto__: Object
status
status changed observer-refactor-code.html:88
what property changed? status observer-refactor-code.html:48
how did it change? update observer-refactor-code.html:49
whats the current value? Status changed observer-refactor-code.html:50

Object observer-refactor-code.html:51
    name: "status"
    object: Object
    oldValue: "Employee Status
    "type: "update"
    __proto__: Object
```

Hot swapping components

In the observer pattern, we have one nice feature, which is called **hot swapping**. With this feature, we can add or delete subscribers at runtime. Let's say we want to monitor a log to fix the issue, then we can easily add log using this pattern without putting down the whole system. Then, we can swap with normal code once the issue is fixed.

Browser compatibility of the observer API

The following screenshot shows us which browser versions support the observer API so that it can help us decide in which version we can test or see our code while we implement the observer pattern:

IE/Edge	Firefox	Chrome	Safari	Opera	IOS Safari	Opera Mini	Android Browser	Chrome for Android
8							4.1	
9		31					42	
10		42					4.3	
11	38	43	7.1		7.1		4.4.4	
Edge	39	44	8	30	8.4	8	40	42
	40	45	9	31	9			
	41	46		32				
	42	47						

Not Supported ▓ Supported

From the mentioned image, we can see that only Chrome and Opera support the observer API.

Summary

In this chapter, you learned about the observer pattern, in which situation we can use the observer pattern, its advantages, disadvantages, and its different types of implementations. At last, we saw the observer pattern with the use of the TDD life cycle.

In the next chapter, you will learn about server-side testing with the use of Node.js in detail.

8
Testing with Server-Side JS

Until now, we have been learning about testing the frontend part of a system. We learned many tools that could test the functions needed to support frontend, feature detection, and so on. In this chapter, we will learn about server-side testing for which we will be using Node.js and Mocha.

We will be covering the following topics in this chapter:

- Setting up the environment
- The server-side JavaScript testing

Setting up the environment

We have covered the simple unit test on the frontend JavaScript with different frameworks in our previous chapters. When it comes to unit testing the code on the server side, we mostly remain unaware of the order in which the functions will be called, we may either try to run the tests in a callback, or we might be interested in checking asynchronous behavior in the functions.

We have lots of frameworks available in the market for testing a server-side code as JUnit, PHPUnit, NUnit, QUnit, Mocha, and other frameworks for server-side code testing. We will use Mocha along with Node.js in this chapter to understand the server side testing with JS. Most of the unit testing frameworks are similar in the features that they provide, and a choice must be made as per the project and the comfort of the team.

In a project, classes are usually models and helper classes contain business logics. For server-side testing, we usually write unit tests for components with business logic. There can also be another scenario where classes interact with other components and databases. Each application has a different workflow, so it's not possible to cover every testing scenario. So, let's start writing our first server-side test with Node.js and Mocha.

Installing Node.js

First, we have to download and install Node.js, if we have not installed it in the system. We can download Node.js from `http://nodejs.org` and follow the instructions mentioned here:

1. Download the installer for your operating system from `http://nodejs.org/`. In this chapter, we will use the windows installer to set up; and thus, we will download the MSI file for the Node.js installer.

2. Run the installer and the MSI file that we downloaded.

3. The installer wizard will ask for your choice of features to be installed; you can select as per your choice. Usually, we install with default choices selected:

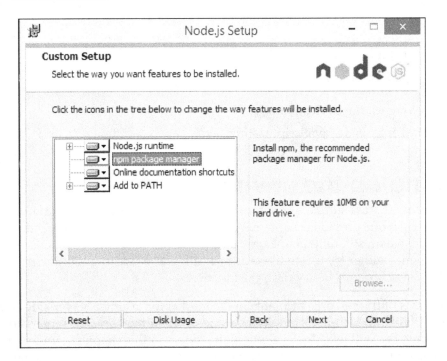

4. If the installation asks for the system restart, then restart your computer.

Once the system is restarted, we can check whether Node.js was set up properly or not. Open the command prompt and run the following command:

```
node --version    // will result something like 2.14.4
```

You should be able to see the version information, which ensures that the installation was successful.

Setting up the application

Let's start with our application on Node.js. Create a directory with the application name of your choice. For the next example, we are going to keep it as `serverside-testing`. Open the command prompt/console and navigate to the directory you created. Run the following command:

npm init

This command will initialize our app and ask several questions to create a JSON file named `package.json`. The utility will ask questions about application name, entry point, test command, description, author name, license information, and so on. After the command is executed, it will generate a `package.json` file in the `application` folder.

```
{
    "name": "serverside-testing",
    "version": "1.0.0",
    "description": "A sample app to test server side JavaScript.",
    "main": "index.js",
    "scripts": {
        "test": "echo \"Error: no test specified\" && exit 1"
    },
    "keywords": [
        "server-side",
        "node.js"
    ],
    "author": "Authors",
    "license": "GPL-3.0"
}
```

For now, we will skip the question of the `test` command (we will add that later). Now, we will add one more file to our folder named `index.js`, which we have defined as an entry point to an application. We're going to leave it blank for now.

Choosing a test runner

There are so many test runners/frameworks available in the market. Out of these, a few are listed here:

- **Nodeunit**: Nodeunit is simple to use; it is a lightweight test runner, which provides asynchronous unit testing for Node.js and browser. Nodeunit supports set up and tear down and mocking and stubbing for unit tests, along with a support for the HTML and jUnit XML reports. You can get Nodeunit at `https://github.com/caolan/nodeunit` at GitHub.

- **Mocha**: Mocha is similar to Nodeunit; it is like a test creation API. Mocha is simple and has rich features such as browser support, asynchronous testing, and so on. It supports a number of assertion libraries out of which you can choose a library of your choice to perform assertions in unit tests. Mocha is available at `https://mochajs.org/`.

- **Vows**: This is a behavior-driven development framework (BDD) to test the asynchronous code for Node.js. It executes your tests in an equivalent manner and sequentially as per your need. Vows is available at `http://vowsjs.org/`.

For this chapter, we will be using Mocha testing framework as it's easy and simple to use from the command line. It reflects the status via exit code and uses **Chai**, which is an excellent replacement for Node's standard assert functions.

Mocha and Chai

Before we start writing a test with Mocha, let's get some more information about Mocha and Chai. Mocha is a testing framework that runs on Node.js. Mocha is simple and has rich features such as browser support, asynchronous testing; it supports a number of assertion libraries.

Mocha's support for multiple assertion libraries allows users to pick one of their choice based on comfort, easiness, and more. Since only the assertion library changes, the test runner output and look and feel stays the same when we run tests.

A complete list of features can be seen at `https://mochajs.org/#features`, which includes more than 20 distinguished features.

Chai is a fairly popular option to use as an assertion library with mocha. Chai is available at `http://chaijs.com/`.

Let's continue with our application. We are going to use some node modules, which are going to help us with unit testing. For unit testing, we will use Mocha. And for this, we would need an assertion library to cater our needs. Chai is a fairly popular option to use as assertion library with Mocha:

```
npm install mocha --save
npm install chai --save
```

 We use the `save` command to save these dependencies in our `package.json` file.

During the server testing phase, we will need a server to send HTTP requests. Also, we will require the EXPRESS package to handle the routing and incoming request. To do this, we need to install the Request and Express package:

```
npm install request --save
npm install express --save
```

Let's also update `package.json` to include a script to run our tests. Update `scripts` in JSON as:

```
"scripts": {
    "test": "mocha --reporter spec"
}
```

This will help us run Mocha for our tests. Whenever we will run our tests, it will run the mentioned script. In this case, it will run `"mocha --reporter spec"`. The `package.json` file will now be similar to the following:

```
{
    "name": "serverside-testing",
    "version": "1.0.0",
    "description": "A sample app to test server side JavaScript.",
    "main": "index.js",
    "scripts": {
        "test": "mocha --reporter spec"
    },
    "keywords": [
        "server-side",
        "node.js"
    ],
    "author": "Authors",
    "license": "GPL-3.0",
    "dependencies": {
        "chai": "^3.3.0",
        "express": "^4.13.3",
        "mocha": "^2.3.3",
        "request": "^2.64.0"
    }
}
```

After installing all needed modules, let's start writing our first test using the existing example of the convert currency module to know about syntax. Let's create a directory named `custom_modules` and a file named `currency-convertor.js` to store our module:

```
var convertCurrency = function(amount,rateOfConversion)
{
    var toCurrencyAmount = 0;

    return toCurrencyAmount;
}
module.exports = convertCurrency;
```

In the preceding code, an empty function is created, which will later contain our production code. We named it `convertCurrency` and exported it as a node module.

Now, we will write a unit test for our module. Let's create a directory inside our app and call it `test`, where we will keep all our tests, and then we will create a JavaScript file named `testCurrencyConversion.js`.

As mentioned before, we are using Chai with Mocha, so first, we have to include Chai by calling the `expect` function. Expect is one of the out-of-box option that comes with the BDD syntax:

```
var expect = require("chai").expect;
var convertCurrency = require("../custom_modules/currency-
convertor.js");
```

Similar to Jasmine as seen in *Chapter 4, Jasmine*, we can use `describe` and `it` with Mocha as well. So, a simple unit test to check whether currency was properly converted or not can be as follows:

```
describe('Convert Currency', function() {
    it('100 INR should be equal to $ 1.59', function() {
        expect(convertCurrency(100, 1/63)).to.equal('1.59');
    });
});
```

We will test using the `it` block, which contains our assertions. The `it` block is very similar to the `describe` function, but we can only put the `expect` function in the body of the `it` function. Following are some of the getters that can be chained with the `expect` function:

Getters	Getters	Getters	Getters
to	be	been	is
that	and	have	with
at	of	same	a
an			

Now, run your test with the command `npm test`. Our test will fail because there was no implementation done yet, as shown in the following screenshot:

```
D:\B04569_Chapter_08\Code\serverside-testing>npm test

> serverside-testing@1.0.0 test D:\B04569_Chapter_08\Code\serverside-testing
> mocha --reporter spec


  Convert Currency
    1) 100 INR should be equal to $ 1.59


  0 passing (20ms)
  1 failing

  1) Convert Currency 100 INR should be equal to $ 1.59:
     AssertionError: expected 0 to equal '1.59'
      at Context.<anonymous> (D:\B04569_Chapter_08\Code\serverside-testing\test\testCurrencyConversion.js:6:41)
      at callFn (D:\B04569_Chapter_08\Code\serverside-testing\node_modules\mocha\lib\runnable.js:286:21)
      at Test.Runnable.run (D:\B04569_Chapter_08\Code\serverside-testing\node_modules\mocha\lib\runnable.js:279:7)
      at Runner.runTest (D:\B04569_Chapter_08\Code\serverside-testing\node_modules\mocha\lib\runner.js:421:10)
      at D:\B04569_Chapter_08\Code\serverside-testing\node_modules\mocha\lib\runner.js:528:12
      at next (D:\B04569_Chapter_08\Code\serverside-testing\node_modules\mocha\lib\runner.js:341:14)
      at D:\B04569_Chapter_08\Code\serverside-testing\node_modules\mocha\lib\runner.js:351:7
      at next (D:\B04569_Chapter_08\Code\serverside-testing\node_modules\mocha\lib\runner.js:283:14)
      at Immediate._onImmediate (D:\B04569_Chapter_08\Code\serverside-testing\node_modules\mocha\lib\runner.js:319:5)

npm ERR! Test failed.  See above for more details.
```

We use the `D:\B04569_Chapter_08\Code` directory to store our applications. We have created an application directory `serverside-testing`, which will contain all our code and needed directories (`custom_modules`, `test`, `app`, and more).

Let's put some implementation to our module:

```
var convertCurrency = function(amount,rateOfConversion)
{
    var toCurrencyAmount = 0;
    // conversion
```

```
    toCurrencyAmount = rateOfConversion * amount;
    // rounding off
    toCurrencyAmount = parseFloat(Math.round(toCurrencyAmount *
                                 100) / 100).toFixed(2);
    return toCurrencyAmount;
}
module.exports = convertCurrency;
```

Now, let's run the tests again. You will see that your tests pass successfully:

```
D:\B04569_Chapter_08\Code\serverside-testing>npm test

> serverside-testing@1.0.0 test D:\B04569_Chapter_08\Code\serverside-testing
> mocha --reporter spec


Convert Currency
  √ 100 INR should be equal to $ 1.59


1 passing (20ms)
```

As you can see, it shows that our tests passed. It will show the amount of time it took to run the tests, and the details about how many tests passed or failed.

Server-side unit testing

In the previous example, we saw a way to start and run our test in Mocha. Server-side testing is important, because it helps you to know your code quality, speed, services request, and response time.

Implementing the web server

For a server-side support, we need to implement an HTTP server, which will serve our requests. Follow the points here to add a web server in our application:

1. Create a subdirectory called app with an index.html file inside. Leave the index.html file blank as of now.

2. Create a file inside the test directory named testMyapp.js.

3. Create a file `app.js` to add our application code. The `serverside-testing` application directory structure will now look like this:

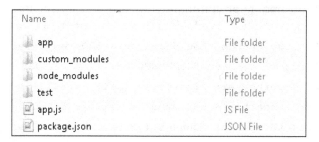

Name	Type
app	File folder
custom_modules	File folder
node_modules	File folder
test	File folder
app.js	JS File
package.json	JSON File

4. Before we write any production code, let's write a test that shows your server running status in `testMyapp.js`. First, we need to load the following modules that we need in our tests:

```
var assert = require("chai").assert;
var http   = require("http");
```

 The `http` module: with the help of this module requests can be sent to server on the specified port.

5. We will load the module app and assign it to a variable named `server`. Next, we will define the Mocha's `describe` function to describe the test that we are about to implement. After this, we add `it` that represents the body of the description:

```
describe('Testing Running Status of Server', function() {
    it("should return a 200 response", function (done) {

        http.get("http://localhost:8000", function
        (response) {
            assert.equal(response.statusCode, 200);
            done();
        });
    });
});
```

6. In the `it` block, we call the function that was returned from the module. This will start the static server. Then, we will call `http.get()` and provide a callback function. Inside this, we will assert a module to check the server response as `200`.

7. After the assertion, we called `done()`, which is a Mocha function asking Mocha to wait for asynchronous operations.

8. Now, run the `npm test` command and you will see the test failed since there is no server object available. We will get an error like this:

```
Server Running Status should return a 200 response:

Uncaught Error: connect ECONNREFUSED 127.0.0.1:8000

at Object.exports._errnoException (util.js:837:11)

at exports._exceptionWithHostPort (util.js:860:20)

at TCPConnectWrap.afterConnect [as oncomplete] (net.js:1060:14)
```

9. The test failed because we have not created an `app` module yet. Now, we'll create a tiny module that will create a static web server using `express`, and point it at the `app` directory. Add the following lines to the module file named `server.js` in the `custom_modules` directory:

```
var express = require("express");
var path    = require("path");
var http    = require("http");
```

- The `express` module is used to handle the routing and incoming request

- The `path` module contains utilities for handling and transforming file paths:

```
module.exports = function () {
    var base = path.resolve("app"); // pointing the app
                                              directory
    var app = express().use(express.static(base)); //
                                              starts app
    return http.createServer(app).listen(8000); // using
                                              port 8000
};
```

- `module.exports` is the object that contains the result of a `require` call. We will point the `app` directory to resolve all the paths. By default, it will look for the `index.html` that we created. Our updated test will include the module that we just created:

```
var assert = require("chai").assert;
var http   = require("http");

var server = require("../custom_modules/server.js");

describe('Testing Running Status of Server', function() {
    it("should return a 200 response", function (done) {
```

```
var app = server(); // creates a server
http.get("http://localhost:8000", function
(response) {
    assert.equal(response.statusCode, 200);
    done();
});
        });
    });
});
```

10. Now, run the `npm test` command, and you will see your test pass in the green info:

```
> mocha --reporter spec

Convert Currency
    √ 100 INR should be equal to $ 1.59

Server Running Status
    √ should return a 200 response (69ms)

2 passing (96ms)
```

In the next steps, we will perform the server-side testing, which also involves database.

Helpdesk – sample application

We will create a small application for performing a server-side testing. This application is based on the helpdesk ticket tracking tool, where users can log in and raise helpdesk tickets online. Every user can see the status of the ticket in the user dashboard.We will need some modules to create the applications. They are listed here:

- **Node.js**: Node.js is the core of our application. It is used to write event-driven programs, which are scalable in nature.

- **Express@3.x**: This is an HTTP utility and acts as a middleware.

- **MongoDB**: The MongoDB Node.js driver is used as a database of the application.

- **Mongoose**: This is the MongoDB object modeling tool to work in an asynchronous environment.

- **Swig**: This is a JavaScript Template Engine to render our dynamic HTML.

These are the some major modules that we use in our application along with the other npm modules. Installing any module with npm command always uses --save at the end of the command using this will update the package.json file of an application.

Let's add the production code to app.js, which will start the server whenever the app runs:

```
var port = 8000;

var server = app.listen(port, function() {
  console.log('Server started, listening to the port - :', port);
});
```

We will also need to include several other modules:

```
var express = require('express');

// custom modules
var user = require('./custom_modules/user');
var TicketDetail = require('./custom_modules/ticket');

var http = require('http');
var cons = require('consolidate'), name = 'swig';
var path = require('path'); // to resolve paths
var passport = require('passport');
var LocalStrategy = require('passport-local').Strategy;
var mongoose = require('mongoose/'); // modeling tool for MongoDB
var methodOverride = require('method-override');
var mongodb = require('mongodb');
```

We will keep adding the production code to our app.js file as we go on with the chapter.

Setting up the MongoDB database

We will use MongoDB for our database, where we will store the data required by the application. First, we have to download the MongoDB setup from https://www.mongodb.com/ and then follow these steps:

1. Download the package as per the available version for your operating system. For Windows, we have to download mongodb-win32-x86_64-enterprise-windows-64-3.0.6-signed.msi.

2. Run your Installer Wizard, accept the license, and select the complete installation when prompted:

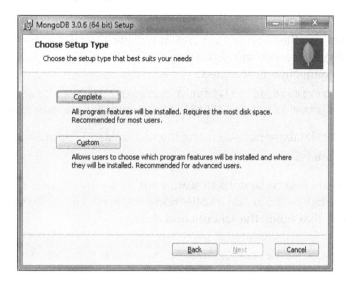

3. After installation, open the `mongodb` directory and go to the `bin` folder.

4. Open the command prompt and run the following command to set the database path. Choose the path as per your setup:

```
mongod --dbpath D:\B04569_Chapter_08\Code\serverside-testing\data
```

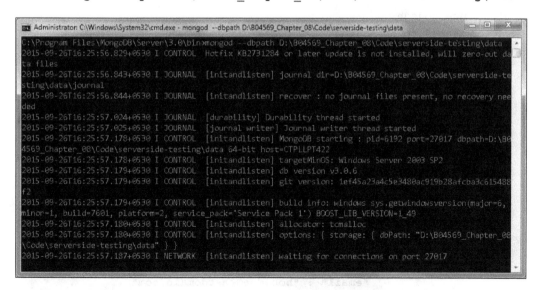

Running the previous command will start a server and wait for connections.

5. Then, open a new command window in the same directory and type mongo to connect with your database:

```
mongo
```

6. Once you run the mongo command, it will start the database connection, and the MongoDB server will show you the following line, which acknowledges that the connection is accepted:

```
2015-09-26T16:26:48.787+0530 I NETWORK   [initandlisten] connection
accepted from 127.0.0.1:36433 #1 (1 connection now open)
```

7. Create the database nodedb using the use nodedb command:

```
use nodedb
```

8. Now, create two collections to store your data — UserDetails and TicketDetails. To create a collection for UserDetails, let's create a variable that holds the schema and data:

```
user = [
{ "username" : "alice","password":"secret","name":"Alice
Doe",       "email" : "alice.doe@testdomain.com" },
{ "username" : "bob","password":"secret","name":"Bob Doe",
   "email" : "bob.doe@testdomain.com" }
]
```

9. In the user object, we have username, password, name, and e-mail. Run the following commands to create a variable user:

```
> use nodedb
switched to db nodedb

> users =
[
        {

                "username" : "alice",
                "password" : "secret",
                "name" : "Alice Doe",
                "email" : "alice.doe@testdomain.com"
        },
        {

                "username" : "bob",
                "password" : "secret",
                "name" : "Bob Doe",
                "email" : "bob.doe@testdomain.com"

        }
];
```

10. The previous command created a variable `user`, which holds the information of two users. We can now insert these into collections:

```
> db.users.insert(user);
BulkWriteResult({
        "writeErrors" : [ ],
        "writeConcernErrors" : [ ],
        "nInserted" : 2,
        "nUpserted" : 0,
        "nMatched" : 0,
        "nModified" : 0,
        "nRemoved" : 0,
        "upserted" : [ ]
})
```

11. We created a new collection `users` in `db`. Similarly, we can create tickets collection:

```
> tickets =
[
        {
                "user" : "",
                "email" : "",
                "issuetype" : "",
                "department" : "",
                "ticketstate" : "",
                "comments" : "",
                "createddate" : ""
        }
];
> db.tickets.insert(tickets);
BulkWriteResult({
        "writeErrors" : [ ],
        "writeConcernErrors" : [ ],
        "nInserted" : 1,
        "nUpserted" : 0,
        "nMatched" : 0,
        "nModified" : 0,
        "nRemoved" : 0,
        "upserted" : [ ]
})
```

Now, we have our data ready to use in the application.

The Mocha test

In our application, we will have multiple modules to perform our operations. Here is the list of the modules that we have included in our test:

- Login
- Dashboard
- Add ticket
- Logout

The flow of login typically goes like the following figure. First, users will land on the login page and try to log in. If the login is successful, users are redirected to the dashboard.

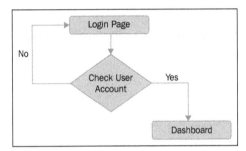

Users should be able to log in from the browser using the login page. When a user is properly authenticated, he/she will be able to see the dashboard. After the login, the user will also be able to add tickets.

 You can copy the application from code files for this chapter.

Let's start developing our application further by adding the user.js file to custom_modules, which we will use to create our UserDetails module:

```
var mongoose = require('mongoose');
var Schema = mongoose.Schema;
var passportlocal = require('passport-local');

var UserDetail = new Schema({
    username: String,
    name: String,
    password: String,
    email: String
    }, {
```

```
        collection: 'users'
    });
var UserDetails = mongoose.model('users', UserDetail);

module.exports = UserDetails;
```

Similarly, we add a `ticket.js` file that we will use for the `TicketDetail` module:

```
var mongoose = require('mongoose');
var Schema = mongoose.Schema;
var passportlocal = require('passport-local');

var addTicketSchema = new Schema({
    user: String,
    email: String,
    issuetype : String,
    department : String,
    ticketstate : String,
    comments : String,
    createddate : Date
}, {
        collection: 'tickets'
    });

var TicketDetail = mongoose.model('tickets', addTicketSchema);

module.exports = TicketDetail;
```

Open `testMyapp.js` from the `test` directory. Add the required modules in your test:

```
var userlogin = require('../routes/user');
var mongoose = require('mongoose');
var db;
```

We test the login module first so we have added user login module in our test and also we have included `mongoose` to connect our database with MongoDB.

Just like other unit testing tools, Mocha also provides the `setUp` and `tearDown` functions in the form of the `before()`, `after()`, `beforeEach()`, and `afterEach()` hooks. These hooks can be asynchronous as well, which look like a regular test case:

```
before(function() {
  // runs before all tests
});
after(function() {
```

```
// runs after all tests
  });
  beforeEach(function() {
    // runs before each test
  });
  afterEach(function() {
    // runs after each test
  });
```

In the `Before` statement, we will define a database connection so that we can use that connection to perform the `db` operations:

```
before(function(done) {
    db = mongoose.connect('mongodb://localhost:27017/nodedb');
                                        // creates connection
    done();
});
```

We will use the port number `27017`, which is a default port by the `mongodb` instance installed. `nodedb` is the database name that we created in the `mongodb` instance. In case you are testing a remote MongoDB server, you will change the hostname, port, and database name accordingly. For testing asynchronous code, Mocha provides you the callback method `done()`. By adding `done()`, it will wait for things to complete before everything else happens in the following blocks:

```
after(function(done) {
        mongoose.connection.close(); // closes connection.
        done();
});
```

Once all the tests are run, we can close the connection:

```
beforeEach(function(done) {
        var user = new userlogin({
            username: 'testuser',
            password: 'test'
        });

        user.save(function(error) {
            if (error) console.log('Error while saving user -' +
                                    error.message);
            else console.log('no error in saving a new user');
            done();
        });
});
```

The `beforeEach` hook will run before each test execute. In this block, we will use the `user` module to create a dummy username and password to save it to the database:

```
afterEach(function(done) {
    userlogin.remove({username: 'testuser'}, function() {
if (error) console.log('Error while removing user -' +
error.message);
    else console.log('user remove from the database
    successfully'); done();
    });
});
```

The `afterEach` hook will run after all the tests complete their execution. In this block, we used the `user` module to create a dummy user with the username `testuser` and password `test`, and save it on the database.

Now, let's update our `app.js` file in order to connect with MongoDB:

```
var MongoClient = mongodb.MongoClient;
mongoose.connect('mongodb://localhost:27017/nodedb');
var db = mongoose.connection;
db.on('error', console.error.bind(console, 'Error while connecting
mongodb :'));
db.once('open', function (callback) {
  // Ha, connection opens!
});
```

Now, let's add some tests for the application. First, we need to check if we are getting the correct login page when the server is hit for the first time in the browser:

```
it("should return the login page ", function (done) {
        var url = "http://localhost:8000";
        http.get(url, function (response) {

            var htmlData;
            response.on("data", function (data) {
                htmlData = data;
            }).on("end", function () {
             assert.isTrue(htmlData.indexOf
             ("<title>Login</title>") != -1);
                done();
            });
        });
    });
```

In the preceding code, we checked whether the page has Login as its title or not. Let's add the login-related logic to app.js:

```
app.get('/', function (request, response, next) {
    response.render('login');
});
app.get('/login', function (request, response, next) {
    response.render('login');
});

app.post('/login',
  passport.authenticate('local', {
    successRedirect: '/dashboard',
    failureRedirect: '/loginFailure'
  })
);

app.get('/loginFailure', function(request, response, next) {
  response.render('login', {msg:'Authentication Failed.Please
  enter valid user credentials',show:'alert alert-danger'});
});
```

Delete the index.html file that we previously created in the app directory. It's not needed now when a user lands with http://localhost:8000.

If you run the application now, you will be able to see a login page as follows:

If you notice, we have added `passport.authenticate()` in the `app.post()` method. The `passport` module allows us to authenticate users. We have mentioned that the user will redirect to `/dashboard` if the authentication turns out successfully, otherwise it will redirect to the `/loginFailure` path:

```
passport.use(new LocalStrategy(function(username, password, done)
{
  process.nextTick(function() {
    user.findOne({
      'username': username,
    }, function(err, user) {
      if (err) {
        return done(err);
      }

      if (!user) {
        return done(null, false);
      }

      if (user.password != password) {
        return done(null, false);
      }

      return done(null, user);
    });
  });
}));
// serialize user
passport.serializeUser(function(user, done) {
  done(null, user);
});
// deserialize user
passport.deserializeUser(function(user, done) {
  done(null, user);
});
```

Let's run your test with `npm test` command to see the results:

```
D:\B04569_Chapter_08\Code\serverside-testing>npm test
> serverside-testing@1.0.0 test D:\B04569_Chapter_08\Code\serverside-testing
> mocha --reporter spec

Listening on port: 8000
  Convert Currency
    √ 100 INR should be equal to $ 1.59

  Server Running Status
GET / 200 81.912 ms - 1746
    √ should return a 200 response (118ms)

  Testing Login Module
connection error: { [Error: Trying to open unclosed connection.] state: 1 }
no error in saving a new user
GET / 200 4.971 ms - 1746
    √ should return the correct page LOGIN
user remove from the database successfully
  3 passing (257ms)
```

We get a MongoDB connection error, because our app is running on the same connection and we are opening unclosed connection with `connect()`. `connect()` opens the default connection to the db. Since we want two different connections, we need `createConnection()` in the place of `connect()` in `before()`. Now, run the test again and see the results:

```
D:\B04569_Chapter_08\Code\serverside-testing>npm test
> serverside-testing@1.0.0 test D:\B04569_Chapter_08\Code\serverside-testing
> mocha --reporter spec

Listening on port: 8000
  Convert Currency
    √ 100 INR should be equal to $ 1.59

  Server Running Status
GET / 200 78.911 ms - 1746
    √ should return a 200 response (115ms)

  Testing Login Module
no error in saving a new user
GET / 200 5.274 ms - 1746
    √ should return the correct page LOGIN
user remove from the database successfully
  3 passing (257ms)
```

If you see in logs, we have got two messages of our asynchronous code in the database along with passing tests.

We also need to check if the user is already present. Let's now write another test to check whether a user with a given username is already present:

```
it('find a user by username', function(done) {
        userlogin.findOne({ username: 'testuser' },
        function(err, user) {
      user.username.should.eql('testuser');
      console.log("username: ", user.username)
   done();
  });
});
```

For this test, we use `user.username.should.eql()` for which we need to add the `should` module. If we run the tests now, it will pass. This is just another assertion library that we use for this test.

Now, we will write a test to check whether the username exists in our database or not. Mocha allows you to use an assertion library of your choice. We will use `should.js`, node's regular assert module in the test.

If we run our tests, it will pass all the tests.

There are many ways to find a data according to a query our database of users. We'll need a specific user, all users, similar users, and many more different scenarios. Here are a few specific methods:

```
user.find();  // get all the users
user.find({ username: 'username' }) ; // get the user by username
user.findById(1); // get a user with ID of 1
```

We can also use the MongoDB query syntax:

```
user.find({ username: 'username'  }).where('created_at')
.gt(monthAgo)
   .exec();
user.findOneAndUpdate({ username: 'OldUsename' }, { username:
'NewUsername' }
user.findByIdAndUpdate(2, { username: 'NewUsername }
user.findOneAndRemove({ username: 'username'  });
user.findByIdAndRemove(2);
```

Now, if you try to log in with a user that we inserted into the mongodb user collection while setting up mongodb collections, the application will authenticate. If incorrect username and passwords are provided, you will see an error message:

Now, we will test our dashboard URL and check that it should not be accessed directly in browser without a login. Add the following describe block to our testMyapp.js file:

```
describe('Users are required to login before accessing
Dashboard.', function() {
    it("Users must not access dashboard without login.", function
        (done) {

    http.get('http://localhost:8000/dashboard', function
    (response) {
    assert.equal(response.statusCode, 200); // should fail
            done();
        });
    });
});
```

If we run this test, it will prompt assertion error because it can not be 200, if working correctly.

```
1) Required Login to access the Dashboard URL You cannot access the page without login:
    Uncaught AssertionError: expected 302 to equal 200
        at ClientRequest.<anonymous> (D:\B04569_Chapter_08\Code\serverside-testing\test\testMyapp.js
        at HTTPParser.parserOnIncomingClient [as onIncoming] (_http_client.js:415:21)
        at HTTPParser.parserOnHeadersComplete (_http_common.js:88:23)
        at Socket.socketOnData (_http_client.js:305:20)
        at readableAddChunk (_stream_readable.js:146:16)
        at Socket.Readable.push (_stream_readable.js:110:10)
        at TCP.onread (net.js:523:20)
```

The test fails because we cannot access the page without logging in. It always returns `302` as a status code, since we are trying to access the dashboard page without logging in. Let's change the status code to `200` from `302` with a message. If we run the tests now, all the tests will pass again.

If you log into the application with a correct username and password, you will be able to land on the dashboard page where you have options to add tickets:

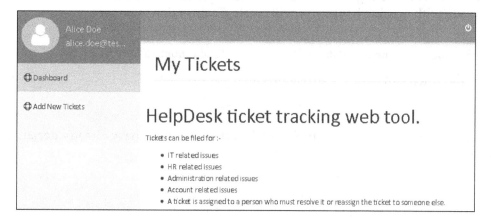

Our next test is based on the ticket module, which will allow us to add tickets. There is a link in the left panel **Add New Tickets** on the dashboard. You will be able to see a form to enter a ticket's details if you click on it:

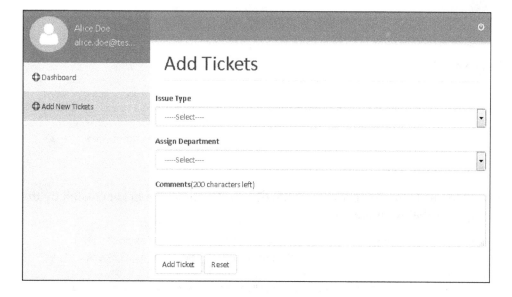

In our test, we will add one ticket in our database and find the tickets according to the users who have submitted the request. We have already added our `TicketDetails` module, which is required to test whether a ticket can be added successfully or not. Add this line with other modules that were included earlier:

```
var TicketDetails = require('./custom_modules/ticket');
```

So now we will be using hooks for testing the asynchronous code. So, we can add new code with existing hooks. We will create a connection in `before()`:

```
db =
mongoose.createConnection('mongodb://localhost:27017/nodedb');
```

In `after()`, we will close the db connection:

```
mongoose.connection.close();
```

In `beforeEach()`, we will add predefined values, which we have already declared in the `ticketDetail` module schema:

```
var ticket = new TicketDetails({
            user: 'testuser',
            email: 'test@testdomain.com',
            issuetype : 'Access Related Issue',
            department : 'IT',
            ticketstate : 'Open',
            comments : 'not able to access the shared database
            URL',
            createddate : Date('2015-8-15')
        });
```

We also need to save data in `before()`:

```
ticket.save(function(error) {
            if (error) console.log('Error while saving a new
            ticket :  ' + error.message);
            else console.log('no error in saving a new
                        ticket);
        });
```

Once all the tests run in `afterEach()`, we should remove the ticket created by the dummy user that we added in `before()`:

```
TicketDetails.remove({user:'testuser'}, function(error) {
    if (error) console.log('Error while removing a ticket:  ' +
    error.message);
                else console.log("ticket removed successfully');
    });
```

Now, we need to add the `it()` block, which will contain assertions of the test. We will test to find a ticket added by the user. So, our complete `describe()` suite will be as follows:

```
describe('Testing ticket module.', function() {
    before(function(done) {
        db =
        mongoose.createConnection
        ('mongodb://localhost:27017/nodedb');
        done();
    });
    after(function(done) {
        mongoose.connection.close(); // closes the connection.
        done();
    });
    beforeEach(function(done) {
        var ticket = new TicketDetails({
            user: 'testuser',
            email: 'test@testdomain.com',
            issuetype : 'Access Related Issue',
            department : 'IT',
            ticketstate : 'Open',
            comments : 'not able to access the shared database
            URL',
            createddate : Date('2015-09-15')
        });
    Ticket.save('Adding a Ticket', function(error) {
        if (error) console.log('Error while saving a ticket -:
        ' + error.message);
        else console.log('no error in saving a new ticket');
    });
        done();
    });
    afterEach(function(done) {
        TicketDetails.remove({user: 'testuser'}, function(error) {
            if (error) console.log('Error while removing a ticket
            :  ' + error.message);
            else console.log('Ticket removed successfully');

        });
        done();
    });
    it('Find tickets of user by email address', function(done) {
        TicketDetails.find({ email: 'test@testdomain.com' },
        function(err, TicketDetails) {
```

```
            TicketDetails.email.should.eql('test@testdomain.com');
            console.log("Email address of user : ",
            TicketDetails.email)

        });
        done();
    });
});
```

Let's run the tests after adding this suite to our testMyapp.js file in the
test directory:

```
> mocha --reporter spec
Listening on port: 8000
  Convert Currency
    ✓ 100 INR should be equal to $ 1.59

  Server Running Status
GET / 200 155.602 ms - 1746
    ✓ should return a 200 response (220ms)

  Testing Login Module
no error in saving a new user
GET / 200 9.993 ms - 1746
    ✓ should return the correct page LOGIN (39ms)
user remove from the database successfully
no error in saving a new user
username:  test090
    ✓ find a user by username
user remove from the database successfully

  Required Login to access the Dashboard URL
GET /dashboard 302 7.503 ms - 28
    ✓ You cannot access the page without login

  Testing ticket module.
    ✓ find a tickets of that user by email

  6 passing (585ms)
```

All our tests passed successfully. Mocha also provides you the time taken by
every test. In this test, the server response time (in milliseconds) is shown in
small brackets ().

Now, users can add new tickets using the **Add Tickets** page:

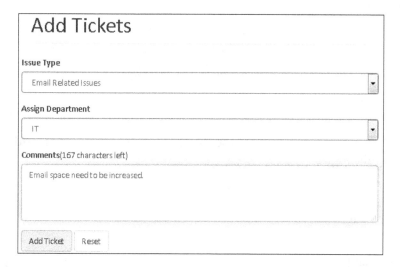

If the ticket is added successfully, you will see the following success message:

Once the ticket is added, it will be displayed on your dashboard:

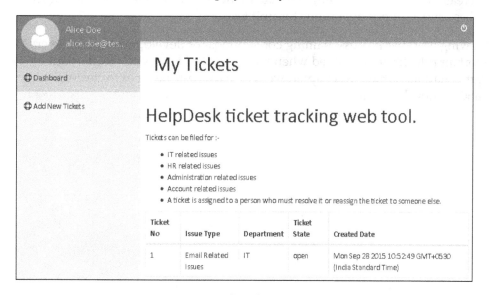

Now, we will write the last test to check if the logged out user returns back to the login page or not:

```
it("must return login page after logout", function (done) {
        http.get(url + '/logout', function (response) {
            expect(url).to.eql(url)
            done();
        });
});
```

Run your test again and you will see the that test passes, because you added the logic while writing the login:

```
app.get('/logout', function(request, response) {
    request.logout();
    response.redirect('/');
});
```

This ensures that the application that we designed for the helpdesk works properly. A helpdesk application is not limited to only these functions, but way more than we added. However, this should give you a view of how to work with the server-side JavaScript application in the test-driven development environment.

Summary

You learned about testing server-side JavaScript using Mocha, and Chai in this chapter. We developed a simple application where users can log in to see dashboard and create tickets while keeping the data in MongoDB. You learned how Mocha handles asynchronous operations for unit tests.

Following a proper process, naming conventions for development plays a very important role. It's more valued when we say that test cases act as alternative documentation. In the next chapter, we will learn best practices for test-driven JavaScript development.

9
Best Practices

From the start of this book, you have been learning concepts of test-driven development for JavaScript along with many tools and frameworks. We got to know about the observer pattern, feature detection, server-side testing, and so on. You learned a number of ways to write unit tests. Knowing how to write unit tests and developing projects is not enough. We need to get the best out of them by following a right process and standard, sometimes referred to as best practices.

In this chapter, you will learn about best practices in JavaScript for test-driven development. We will see different ways that can help us to write good code using test-driven development.

TDD best practices

A **unit test** is a function or method, which invokes a unit of module in software and checks assumptions about the system that the developer has in mind. Unit test helps the developer to test the logical functionality of any module.

In other words, a unit is the testable piece of software. It can have more than one input and normally a single output. Sometimes, we treat a module of a system as a unit.

Unit test is only relevant to developers who are closely working with the code. A unit test is only applicable to test logical piece of the code. Illogical code would not be tested with the use of unit testing. For example, getting and setting values in the text field will not be considered in logical code.

Usually, first unit test is harder to write for any developer. First test requires more time for any developer. We should always ask questions before writing the initial unit test. For example, should you use an already available unit test framework or write your own custom code? What about an automated build process? How about collecting, displaying, and tracking unit test code coverage? Developers are already less motivated to write any unit tests, and having to deal with these questions only makes the process more painful.

Follow proper rules to define test cases

Properly defined test cases gives a better view of the code, and developers can easily find what they want to find in the code. Many tools also need proper naming conventions to be followed. There are so many naming conventions techniques available out of which we will see a few techniques. It is better to follow some naming conventions than nothing, like the saying "something is better than nothing."

Let's take an example of a project. If it is mandatory for all users to follow the same naming conventions, everyone will have to follow the same standard. When it comes to module integration or to understand the code written by other developers, it's easier to follow the flow of system.

Make test case names more readable

The main benefit of following this practice is that it avoids packaging test code with production packages. Even many build tools want us to specify tests in some specific source directory to identify test at runtime. Make sure that you created two source directories. One for source and the other to keep unit test cases. The directory names can be different and as per the frameworks/tool used, for example, Jasmine uses spec for the `tests` directory.

Keep the same name for test files and source files

One commonly used practice is to name tests the same as the source files with the suffix or prefix `Test`. If, for example, the source file is `CurrencyConverter`, the test file should be `CurrencyConverterTest`. Many times it happens that test file is bigger than the main source file, as we can write many test suites for one implementation. For example, if `CurrencyConverter` has a method `convert`, there can be a method in test file with the name `CurrencyConverterConvertTest`.

If the implementation for a source file is to be updated, tests files are updated first. This practice helps users to find the tests written for a source file very easily because of similar names. It should be good to keep the path also the same for source and test to make it easy for any developer. For example, if the source is in `/js/currencycode`, then the test should be in `/test/currencycode`.

Keep the name descriptive

Let's take an example to understand this. If we are going to test a function named CurrencyConverter, we will create a test for this function with the name tCC (thinking that t is for test, C for currency, and last C for converter). During the time when we are working on this function, it will be easy to remember for a day or two, but will you be able to find and identify the source by looking at test. I think it's hard to find.

Advantage of this practice is that anybody can easily understand the objective of implementation. Descriptive names can help identifying the method, which is failing at the time of running the test. We can even take a decision to increase the coverage easily based on descriptive names. We should be clear about the code snippet that we need to run before the test, or if we want to execute any event or actions, and last but not least is the expected outcome. There are many different ways to name test methods, but follow only the ones that are correct as per coding standards.

Applying proper processes

In *Chapter 1, Overview of TDD*, and *Chapter 2, Testing Concepts*, you learned about the TDD life cycle. Processes mentioned in the following section will be helpful to make successful implementation of TDD.

Making sure that tests are written before starting implementation

It is an extremely helpful practice to write test cases for all the requirements before the code is implemented, as it ensures that the code, hence implemented, covers all the requirements. This process helps to understand requirements in details to any developer before starting coding for respective module. Understanding the requirements in detail, will make sure that the implementation done for any module is accurate and properly written.

Let's take an example of change request for any project. In that case, we should first write a test before starting the implementation so that we will get an idea of the number of existing requirements that a change request is affecting. If this is not followed properly, then we are also violating the TDD life cycle, which we understood in *Chapter 2, Testing Concepts*.

Modifying/writing new code only when the test is failing

The most important advantage of following this process is that the developer can be sure that implementation for this particular test has been already written or the test has some defect. This test should be written in such a way that it covers functionality, and if that functionality doesn't exist, then it will fail. We need to be sure that test is verifying the right thing. We can get high confidence by getting the expected output by running all our tests successfully.

Running all the tests when we modify anything in the existing code

We can be sure that by changing the code, we have not broken any existing functionality, which was in working condition before changing the code. Whenever we change anything in the implementation, all our tests cases should run successfully. More often, tests cases should be faster to execute and it should be written in such a way so that any developer can run on their local system.

Ideally, when we have more than one team member carrying out development for any project, we maintain a version control system to maintain changes in the code so that nobody encounters an issue of overwriting code of each other. Many organizations run continuous integration toll after pushing code in version control system to make sure that the code is compiled properly once anybody has pushed it in version control.

Existing tests should pass before new tests are written

The main benefit of this process is to maintain focus on requirements, which were discussed and signed off. Make sure that the implementation code doesn't have major modification. At any stage if we add a new functionality, then it's always good to test the existing tests before adding new tests into the system so that we don't keep some tasks pending in one module and jump on other functionality.

If processes are not followed properly, generally, developers start writing code immediately once after any proposal is signed. They don't acquire proper understanding of the requirement, but just focus on the development. In such cases, we end up in a situation where time lines get stretched for the entire delivery.

During the proposal, organization will realize that their budget is overrunning for the assignment. One mistake in starting creates a bigger problem later. So, it's better to take care from the start and follow proper processes.

Cleaning up code once all test cases are passed

Once we are sure that all functionalities are covered and tests related to functionalities are passed successfully, we can spend time in cleaning up the code to make it more robust and of desired quality. We refactored the code, and now are running test cases to check what the status is. We found that all the test cases are passed, and then relax and feel safe to refactor the code further. After refactoring a few modules, it's better to run test cases once to verify the status of modification. If all the test cases are passed successfully, then we can relax and feel safe to refactor other modules as well. In most cases, adding new test is not needed until major modifications are carried out in requirements; minor modifications to existing tests should be enough. After carrying out cleanup the developer can expect that existing test should pass.

As per the TDD life cycle, we should always refactor the code once we finish implementation of any module so that we will be sure about the good quality of our project.

Follow right development practices

Let's understand right practices to do development using TDD for projects.

Simple code that can be easily understood

This process ensures that our design for the code is easy to understand and clear. This process helps us avoid extra code, which can introduce complexity. The main motive behind keeping the code simple is to make it easy to maintain and better to understand. Complex development ends up in a worst situation, so the key goal for any team member to work for any assignment is to achieve simplicity in design and avoid complex implementation. Walt Whitman, a famous American poet rightly said that "Simplicity is the glory of expression." Many times developers end up writing many lines of code, which can be achieved with few lines. This bad practice adds a complexity in the project for others to understand modules written in bad condition. We should always remember to write code in proper syntax and with good quality.

Writing assertions first

Writing assertions first can provide clarification of the requirement. If assertions are written first, then the purpose for test is clear. Developers need to focus on the code that can accomplish the assertion, and then implementation can be done easily. Assertions can test that our functional requirements are covered with some mocks added in code.

One assertion per test is enough

More often, developers can easily get clarity and understanding if a single assertion requirement is fulfilled. Let's see the ways that can help us follow this practice:

Normally, tests can fail only in one situation, that is, if we don't get the expected behavior. More assertions can end up in a situation of more failures, which makes it difficult to find the root cause of failure. We will not have an idea about all subsequent assertions in test cases in which the first assertion fails. This means that the failure that occurred doesn't represent the exact number of the test suite or state of test suite. In short, we will not be able to get a real picture of the situation! If we find new failures while we are fixing old implementation, it turns into a painful situation.

We should make sure that we define test in an informative and proper way so that if failure occurs, we will get clear picture about it.

When more assertions are added in a test, we think that we have a lot of things to test. Anybody finds it difficult to identify the name of the test when it fails due to multiple assertions. To overcome this situation, we need to provide a name which is proper (to the point), or a name that describes the requirement of the test.

Requirements, in which more than one action is covered, should be tested separately so that if failure or success occurs, we could easily identify from the description of messages.

One test being dependent on other is not an idle situation, and adding more than one assertion in one test is in fact similar to multiple tests, which can be called the **dependency chain**. Tests suites that test the right behavior (give successful result) are of course less dependent on each other. In most cases, where some test fails and others are in an error state, we need to focus on failures and not on the errors.

With all the preceding explanation, we can conclude that a test should be to the point and proper.

In other words, if more than one assertion is added, then it is hard to make a test case more readable. A test with a single assertion is usually easy to read and to the point, and that's an ideal situation!

An example that is simple and easy to explain is stated as follows:

```html
<script>
    function testConvertCurrency(amount, rateOfConversion){
        var toCurrencyAmount = 0;
        // conversion
        toCurrencyAmount = rateOfConversion * amount;
        // rounding off
        toCurrencyAmount =
        Number.parseFloat(toCurrencyAmount).toFixed(2);
        return toCurrencyAmount;
    }
    function testData() {
        assertEquals("Assert
        passed",'1.59',testConvertCurrency(100,1/63));
    }
    function testData1() {
        assertNotEquals("Assert
        Failed",'1.59',testConvertCurrency(100,1/63));
    }
</script>
```

Keep your focus on findability

Concise test names make test suites easy to find. A name with a proper description gives us a good understanding about the code, which is being tested using test and expected output that a developer can expect for a given input. A developer can easily find the scenarios that are not included, by giving proper names. Finally, it can be useful to identify actual errors/problems. Mainly, it happens that everybody has their preference to give names for test, but it is better that we follow the standard rules defined by the frameworks.

Reducing duplication

Mainly, we should always keep a focus on removing duplicate code by putting common code in utility method/files so that we don't put same code at multiple places in our implementation.

There can be a chance of changing the important test while removing duplicate code. We need to keep practice that every time we change anything in the code, we should check tests and see if anything is breaking. If we check after major modifications, then it will be harder to find from where tests are breaking.

Tests should run fast

These days, when browsers are becoming so smart, a project usually has a huge list of functions in JavaScript, and the code is huge. If tests are written properly while following TDD, the number of tests will be high.

We need to make sure that whatever test we write should run fast; otherwise, it can be time consuming and create issues to complete the task on time. In any case, test should not take more time in running it; if that is the case, then developers should not use it and divide it in a small chunk of code and also change the test in small chunk so that the time for running test is lowered.

We are benefited if tests are run fast. Faster feedback and problem detection are two main advantages that any developer can obtain from fast tests. With these two advantages, a developer can fix the problem easily and faster. A developer can easily relate the issue with code easily as it gets detected early.

Using mocks

Mocks are lines of code with some hardcoded behavior and some expectations that we have achieved from the requirement understanding phase. A mock will fail test, if it is not defined as per expectation.

Main benefits of writing mocks are as follows:

- Developers need to spend less time in running test
- If any issue occurs, then it can be fixed easily
- Tests are readable and precise

We will now see an example, which is utilizing a mock:

```
describe("Custom spy object", function(){
    var car;
    before(function(){
        car = jasmine.createSpyObj('car', ['start','stop']);
        car.start();
        car.stop();
    });

    it("Testing if car can be started",function(){
        expect(car.start).toHaveBeenCalled();
    });
    it("Testing if car can be stopped",function(){
```

```
        expect(car.start).toHaveBeenCalled();
    });

});
```

We have seen this example in *Chapter 4, Jasmine*, where we can create a mock using `createSpyObj()`. In the preceding example, we can see that `createSpyObj()` takes two arguments, first is the type or class and second is an array of strings. The passed array of strings is a set of functions for which the spy will be created. In the previous example, a type `car` was created with three spies. All of these spies act as any other spy.

Using stubs

Similar to mocks, stubs are normally used to replace actual implementation of any code. Stubs can be used to execute our implementation in one particular way. We can see how custom code responds for different inputs.

Let's see an example of stub using the following code:

```
it("Spying employee with call through and stub", function(){
    var alice = new Employee("Alice", 4, "Testing");

    spyOn(alice, "calculateSalary").and.callThrough();
    var salary = alice.getSalary();
    console.log("Salary is: "+salary);

    console.log("Now calling stub");
    alice.calculateSalary.and.stub();
    expect(salary).toEqual(4000);
});
```

We created a stub for `calculateSalary` on our employee example.

Using setUp and tearDown methods

The `setUp()` and `tearDown()` methods provide a benefit to run code before and after the execution of test. When you need to set up some data before a test runs, you use the `setUp()` function. Likewise, to clear, delete, and terminate connection tasks which should happen at the end of the test, you use the `tearDown()` function. These functions may have different names in other testing frameworks/tools. Both of these methods are optional, and they will be used only when they are defined.

An example can be used to set some initial data and use the data in the test. Let's check out the following code, which showcases a very simple implementation of the setUp() and tearDown() functions.

Let's see an example of setUp and tearDown methods as follows:

```
<script>
YUI().use('test-console','test', function (Y) {
        var testCase = new Y.Test.Case({
            /*
            * Executes once before running test.
            */
            setUp : function () {
                //Opening a connection code can be added here
            },
            /*
            * Executed after running test.
            */
            tearDown : function () {
                //closing a connection code can be added here
            },
            testData: function () {
                //Connection has been done successfully or not
                    can be tested here
            }
        });

    });
</script>
```

We created a data object, which holds an array in setUp() and deletes the object in tearDown() to free up memory used. Note that setUp() and tearDown() are for data manipulation, actions or assertions should not be used in these functions. Actual implementations and usage would be more complex, but we can still follow the same process. We created an array but any kind of value can be assigned as per the requirements.

Choosing the right tool

In all the previous chapters, we have seen so many tools and frameworks which helped us write unit tests, feature detection, and so on. There are times when one tool is not enough to cater to the needs of a project. We can typically compare these tools based on what they provide because that's what we are interested in. However, we must never overlook the learning path of a tool it may come with for the team.

Feature detection tools

You learned about Modernizr in *Chapter 6, Feature Detection*, which is one of the most popular feature detection libraries. But, it may vary according to the project. In a project, we may need very few tests for features. In that case, sometimes, plain, custom JavaScript code is sufficient to test the features needed.

Sometimes, there are too many rich UI present in the website that it is vital to use a feature detection library such as Modernizr.

Server-side testing tools

Most often server-side code is written using NodeJS, and it's mostly asynchronous. There are a good number of test runners to support NodeJS. A team of developers should use the tool they are familiar with. They should also check for a tool, which has active support by community, tool developers, and so on. We get a brief introduction about NodeUnit, Mocha, Vows for NodeJS test runners. We used Mocha not only because it is popular, but also because it is well supported.

Asynchronous testing

Ajax calls are very often used in any web project. Not all tools can handle frontend Ajax calls very well. We must always check for asynchronous support of a tool before finalizing. Sometimes, if necessary, a proof-of-concept must be developed to see if Ajax calls can be tested easily.

Running time of unit tests

A fast executing code holds focus of developers and encourages them to write better and efficient code. The same concept applies to test cases. You should give preference to a tool, which is fast enough since during TDD, you execute your tests more than your production code. If you calculate by that logic, you need double time for executions in TDD than you need to execute your production code in the normal development approach.

Browser support

A unit testing framework must be able to run successfully on different browsers. Most of the websites are made compatible with all major browsers (Firefox, Internet Explorer, Google Chrome, Safari, Opera, and many more). So, if a unit test performs uniformly on all browsers then that should be a good choice.

Other features

There are more features which can give you a better idea about these tools and frameworks. Let's checkout these features in brief:

- **Nested suites**: No project, these days, is a small when it comes to JavaScript. This leads to a good number of test cases. Grouping them into test suites and further nesting test suites always help to readable and understandable test cases which make sense and act as a perfect documentation.

- **Reporting**: Most of the web projects have requirements which involve reporting. These can be some kind of statistics about visitors, the information users are filling in the forms provided, and so on. Similarly, reporting is also important for test cases. Most of the test runners provide a good way to see reports of failed/passed tests.

- **Code coverage**: Ideally, there should be unit test cases for all of the production code written, but it does not happen every time. Sometimes, it's not possible due to various reasons such as, technical difficulty, lack of time and so on. A testing tool or framework should provide a way to find out the code coverage and to provide the report.

- **Timer support**: Sometimes, we need to wait for some actions to finish and a timer/clock function can help with unit testing of such operations.

- **Build tasks**: Almost all big projects are built using some kind of build tool like Apache Ant, Maven, and many more. Similarly, test cases can also be run using these build tools. Automated builds can check for all unit tests regularly to ensure everything runs fine.

- **IDE supported**: If a tool/framework can be used with a popular IDE like Eclipse, Netbeans, IntelliJ, and so on. An integrated tool helps a faster development and running the tests becomes easy and neat.

- **Support**: Before choosing a framework or tool, its necessary to know if the version being used is still supported or not. Whether it is community supported or supported by its creators. We must know if the tool reached to a stable state or if it was just an experimental version.

- **Customization**: A good tool always allows its users to extend the base capabilities. Custom assertions, custom comparisons, or ability to add new methods can be an example of customization.

- **Mocking**: There are times when you have to deal with the integration of other web services, tools, and so on. While testing, the functions may not be actually available to call and test their output. In such cases, mocking those functions helps a lot. By mocking a function, we can return the desired result and we can continue using that result to test our code further. While mocking, we usually make an assumption that the code being mocked is well tested and works as desired.

- **Dependency**: There are unit testing frameworks which are complete in nature, they have assertion libraries, built-in test runners, and many more. At the other hand, there are just test runners or just assertion libraries. These standalone components need some platform to run upon.

After an analysis of the requirements, you can consider these factors to decide which tool fits for your requirements. Of course, there may be many more factors but this list should be able to help you to some extent.

JsLint

JsLint is used to measure the code quality of JavaScript. We can use that tool to check code compliance with coding rules. It was developed by Douglas Crockford. It provides notifications on error in syntax, any bad practices that are followed in code. Many times syntax errors can break running code in test cases. We think that semicolon or colon is not important in JavaScript, but in some cases that can make a code worse. We are not sure what can happens in worst cases, but it can stop running some test cases.

Summary

Finally, we reached the end of the journey by acquiring better knowledge of why unit testing (TDD) is important for any developer. Developers should realize that a precise and proper test can help them to complete the implementation with a good feeling and better quality. Remember that a bad quality test is as good as not spending any effort on unit testing for any code, so it is better not to write unit test in that condition.

From this chapter, we acquired knowledge about unit testing and TDD. In the software industry, we know that we will only gain knowledge once we get our hands dirty by writing some practical examples. Let's start writing new projects using TDD. Once you are in rhythm, it will be easy to follow and make test-driven development a practice and become a happier and more productive developer. Happy coding!

Index

A

N

V

vendor prefixes 135
Vows
  about 168
  URL 168

W

web pages
  complexity 1, 2
web server
  implementing, in application 172-175

Y

Yahoo User Interface (YUI) 13
yepnope.js
  reference link 125
YUI Test 15

Thank you for buying
Test-Driven JavaScript Development

About Packt Publishing

Packt, pronounced 'packed', published its first book, *Mastering phpMyAdmin for Effective MySQL Management*, in April 2004, and subsequently continued to specialize in publishing highly focused books on specific technologies and solutions.

Our books and publications share the experiences of your fellow IT professionals in adapting and customizing today's systems, applications, and frameworks. Our solution-based books give you the knowledge and power to customize the software and technologies you're using to get the job done. Packt books are more specific and less general than the IT books you have seen in the past. Our unique business model allows us to bring you more focused information, giving you more of what you need to know, and less of what you don't.

Packt is a modern yet unique publishing company that focuses on producing quality, cutting-edge books for communities of developers, administrators, and newbies alike. For more information, please visit our website at www.packtpub.com.

About Packt Open Source

In 2010, Packt launched two new brands, Packt Open Source and Packt Enterprise, in order to continue its focus on specialization. This book is part of the Packt Open Source brand, home to books published on software built around open source licenses, and offering information to anybody from advanced developers to budding web designers. The Open Source brand also runs Packt's Open Source Royalty Scheme, by which Packt gives a royalty to each open source project about whose software a book is sold.

Writing for Packt

We welcome all inquiries from people who are interested in authoring. Book proposals should be sent to author@packtpub.com. If your book idea is still at an early stage and you would like to discuss it first before writing a formal book proposal, then please contact us; one of our commissioning editors will get in touch with you.

We're not just looking for published authors; if you have strong technical skills but no writing experience, our experienced editors can help you develop a writing career, or simply get some additional reward for your expertise.

Jasmine Cookbook

ISBN: 978-1-78439-716-6   Paperback: 276 pages

Over 35 recipes to design and develop Jasmine tests
to produce world-class JavaScript applications

1. A recipe-based approach to design and
    implement Jasmine specs for efficiently
    testing JavaScript jQuery, Ajax, and Fixtures.

2. Implement E2E (end-to-end) scenarios with
    Jasmine Spies and Custom Matchers.

3. Develop Jasmine specs to validate the
    output of a method, object, or unit using
    data-driven approach.

JavaScript Mobile Application Development

ISBN: 978-1-78355-417-1   Paperback: 332 pages

Create neat cross-platform mobile apps using
Apache Cordova and jQuery Mobile

1. Configure your Android, iOS, and Window
    Phone 8 development environments.

2. Extend the power of Apache Cordova
    by creating your own Apache Cordova
    cross-platform mobile plugins.

3. Enhance the quality and the robustness of your
    Apache Cordova mobile application by unit
    testing its logic using Jasmine.

Please check **www.PacktPub.com** for information on our titles

Jasmine JavaScript Testing
Second Edition

ISBN: 978-1-78528-204-1   Paperback: 134 pages

Test your JavaScript applications efficiently using Jasmine and React.js

1. Leverage the power of unit testing React.js to develop full-fledged JavaScript applications.

2. Learn the best practices of modularization and code organization while scaling your application.

3. Enhance your practical skills required to develop applications using the Jasmine framework in a step-by-step manner.

JavaScript Testing Beginner's Guide

ISBN: 978-1-84951-000-4   Paperback: 272 pages

Test and debug JavaScript the easy way

1. Learn different techniques to test JavaScript, no matter how long or short your code might be.

2. Discover the most important and free tools to help make your debugging task less painful.

3. Discover how to test user interfaces that are controlled by JavaScript.

4. Make use of free built-in browser features to quickly find out why your JavaScript code is not working, and most importantly, how to debug it.

Please check **www.PacktPub.com** for information on our titles

www.ingramcontent.com/pod-product-compliance
Lightning Source LLC
Chambersburg PA
CBHW060546060326
40690CB00017B/3624